M000315963

Dedication

In loving memory of my mother, Betty Huntley-Wright

Library of Congress Cataloging-in-Publication Data

McConnel, Bridget.
    The story of the thimble : an illustrated guide for
collectors / Bridget McConnel.
      p. cm.
    Includes bibliographical references.
    ISBN 0-7643-0311-2
    1. Thimbles--Collectors and collecting--Catalogs.
    I. Title.
NK9505.7.M42 1997
646'.19--dc21   97-23818
                                  CIP

Copyright © 1997 by Bridget McConnel

All rights reserved. No part of this work may be reproduced
or used in any form or by any means—graphic, electronic,
or mechanical, including photocopying or information storage and retrieval systems—without written permission from
the copyright holder.

Designed by Bonnie M. Hensley

ISBN: 0-7643-0311-2
Printed in China
1 2 3 4

Published by Schiffer Publishing Ltd.
4880 Lower Valley Road
Atglen, PA 19310
Phone: (610) 593-1777; Fax: (610) 593-2002
E-mail: Schifferbk@aol.com
Please write for a free catalog.
This book may be purchased from the publisher.
Please include $3.95 for shipping.

Please try your bookstore first.
We are interested in hearing from authors
with book ideas on related subjects.

Contents

Acknowledgements

With sincere thanks to the following people who have supplied important information and photographs, some, indeed, of their own private collections. Without all their help this book would not have been as complete and informative as, hopefully, the reader will find it.

Betty Aardewerk
Mrs. G. Abbott
Fredericke Baechle
Mrs. R. Brook
Sonia Cordell
Helen Eastgate
Rosalie Hall
Irja Hesilä
Edwin Holmes
Inez Oaktree
Diane Pelham Burn
Judy Pollitt
Gay-Ann Rogers
Pat Rich
Norma Spicer
Lydia Townsend
Irmgard von Traitteur and all the members
  of the Thimble Society

Organizations and Museums that have been most kind in lending photographs and sending in information are:

The British Museum
The Victoria and Albert Museum
The Petrie Collection at University College
  Museum and the University of Manchester
The Thimble Collectors International / USA

Friends and family who have shown great patience and support from sorting out computer problems to reading proofs and pointing out errors:

Annie Elkins
Josephine and Kenneth Firth
Geoffrey Whitehead
Cavendish Elithorn
Andrea Dekker
Sheila Pusinelli

Introduction

Why would anyone want to collect thimbles? Well, it may help you to know why I did, so this is how it all began. My mother and I had a small general antiques business, because, as a family of actors, artists, and musicians, we often needed to supplement an erratic income. The antique business fitted the bill nicely, it fulfilled our pecuniary needs at the same time as satisfying our artistic interests and there was the bonus of learning history from a personal, practical and often female point of view. Now, in antiques you soon learn that there are many general dealers and collectors, but to specialize is an interesting and more lasting option. The difficulty was deciding what to specialize in. There didn't seem anything that had not already been collected, and that meant little chance of new discoveries and lucky bargains.

I was sitting in the shop, learning the words of a dreadful T.V. script, when I became aware of a very tall, fair-haired man looking down at me while holding a large bundle of wrapped objects. "These are my grandmother's and mother's collection of thimbles and sewing tools and I want to sell them." The bundle was placed on the table and opened with the flourish of a conjuror. Revealed in front of me, in the forms of all sorts of little tools, were continuing generations of women's work. I had little idea of the purpose of most of the implements. I regarded sewing only as a chore, necessary to maintain a hopefully glamorous wardrobe bought from various "Nearly New" shops. All the objects looked so personal, small, ingenious, and very beautifully made, that my intake of breath and reaching out of hands to touch must have demonstrated my delight.

The fair-haired stranger watched me, and probably upped his price at every gasp of pleasure. I will not take up your time with descriptions of all the sewing tools. They will have their own story in my next book to do full justice to their beauty and variety. The grandmother, whose name was Abigail, and the mother whose name was Hannah, certainly had enjoyed collecting thimbles. There were about 100 of them, made from every imaginable material, silver, gold, brass, porcelain, ivory, bone, wood, tortoiseshell, enamel and glass. Some were contained in worn fitted leather boxes, some in silver "acorn" cases, and some hung suspended from a gold chain. The majority were free of any case, having once resided in a sewing box. As I looked more closely at each thimble I was amazed at the fineness and variety of execution in their design and shape. Minute scenic designs appeared on this one, "Forget Me Not" was engraved around another, a tiny exquisite enamel pansy set into mother-of-pearl on a third.

Each thimble was a perfect miniature display of good workmanship, and each set out to charm. No wonder they were considered the perfect gift of a gentleman to a lady. Perhaps what hooked me most was the very personal nature of the object. Many people collect stamps, snuff boxes, and china figures, but for me the thimble seemed to hold the magic of the past in its small enclosure. The fair-haired man must have noticed my interest with pleasure., "£500 for the entire collection," he said. As this was in 1981 it was a "full" price. Moreover, it was more money than the family purse could provide. Well, actors need compassionate bank managers and I had one. The interest rate was not too daunting, so I became the next owner of Abigail and Hannah's thimbles.

Now I was presented with the problem of not knowing anything about my purchase. There was only one thimble book in Britain at the time, *Thimbles* by Edwin Holmes. After I had read that excellent volume, I was on my own. There were very few thimbles in any of the museums and the ones on view were usually accompanied by the largely redundant notice "A collection of thimbles," with no accompanying information. I decided to display them in my shop with the tentative but hopeful addition of "mainly nineteenth century." What happened next was a surprise; within about six weeks a large part of the collection had sold. I had retained what appeared to be the most interesting examples for research purposes, but the main body of silver and metal had flown off like lightning. Even more surprising was that those first customers were coming back for more.

Well, restocking was the hard part, but gradually by word of mouth, more thimbles appeared. They were very few and far between and none of us involved quite knew what we were buying or selling. Prices were solely dependant on what we had paid for something and how much we liked it. I overheard a fellow collector describing some metal examples as "early tip-ware." Why did you call them that? He replied, "when I have no idea what something is, I classify things found on our local tip as 'early tip-ware.' This means I found them before 9 a.m., the middle period is up to 4 p.m., and 'late tip-ware' is anything after 4 p.m." This story has made me laugh for years, and it helps deflate the pomposity that creeps into any field of collecting as knowledge develops.

This lack of information was, however, beginning to be annoying. Here were these intriguing little objects, completely lacking their own story. People who had begun buying them wanted to know more about their history. When was the first thimble made? Did tailors use the same style as seamstresses? What was a Dorcas thimble?... and so on. Letters came to me requesting all sorts of information. In the end it was easier to compile a small newsletter with hand drawn illustrations and ask other collectors to be kind enough to contribute. That was how the Thimble Society was born, and it was mainly from the circulation of the Thimble Society magazine that this book was commissioned.

It seems to me that part of the success of thimble collecting is due to picturing the contemporary setting, and stories attached to thimbles and to the thimble makers. So as well as guiding you through their history, I will tell you some of the stories that I liked best. For example, it appealed to my imagination that the idea of enhancing one's adornment started a long time ago. The earliest sample of any sewn work appears on the clothes of a Cro-Magnon man (c.30,000 BC) excavated in Vladimir, Russia. The fur of his cap and boots had been decorated with sewn ivory beads. Some form of attaching skins must have started long before that, but as far as we know that is the earliest example of sewing using a needle, as opposed to joining clothes together with an awl or bodkin. Of course the type of thimble that you use is governed by the needle, so the two tools often developed together.

Because it is engrossing to see the development of a tool through time, I will guide you through the history of thimbles in chronological order. During what I hope will be an enjoyable perambulation, note that the three most important elements to consider are material, construction, and design, the material being what something is made out of [e.g. silver, wood], the construction being how it was made [e.g. in two parts, or cast], the design being its shape and decoration. The understanding of these three elements will tell you the age and provenance of your thimble. The first element is probably the easiest to master. Normally the look and feel will help you to distinguish various metals, woods, and natural substances such as mother-of-pearl. The construction is best understood if I give you a description alongside a relevant photo as we proceed. The third element, that of design, is probably the most interesting, because it tells you most about when the thimble was made. When there is no hallmark or maker's mark to help you, you can compare the design and ornamentation of other objects of a period, such as silver ware or textiles, with the design on your thimble and that information will help you date it more accurately.

Chapter 1

A Brief Look at the History of Thimbles and Needles

It is useful to have some idea of the earliest known examples of needles, awls, pushers, and thimbles. If we look at some items of sewing together, when you next visit your local museum, you might be able to identify some hitherto odd object that may have baffled the curator. Often in the past archaeologists, historians and museum curators were men, who, naturally enough, possessed very little idea of sewing tools, so items were often incorrectly attributed. This book may give you the confidence to air your knowledge, always good for the ego.

We have already noted the sewn work that appeared on the Cro-Magnon man [c.30,000 BC]. For needles we have to move on to the earliest bone needles that were found in Neolithic cave settlements in France, c.15,000 BC. Similar examples can be seen in the British Museum in London. As yet there is no example of any kind of needle pusher; perhaps a skin pad was used. There is then a further gap of 5000 years until our first needle pusher appears. Dating from approximately 10,000 BC, Neolithic sites in Europe, Africa and China have yielded pushers or Acutrudia made of stone. They appear very reminiscent of a sailor's palm. The accompanying needles were probably made out of wood and porcupine quills as well as bone.

The next important period, showing a great change in the level of sophistication in society, takes us forward another 5000 years to ancient Egypt. By 5000 BC there was a thriving weaving and textile industry along the fertile banks of the Nile. Men and women were beginning to develop a taste for luxury, where previously only survival had been sought. The ancient Egyptian culture still casts its web of fascination over us today. A greater understanding of the everyday life of the Ancient Egyptians has given us a better picture of a colorful, humorous, very civilized people with advanced scientific understanding and many tools to support the technology needed for such a powerful nation to maintain its supremacy.

The textile industry, based on linen made from flax, was in evidence as early as the Fayum A culture of 5000 BC. There are many pictorial records found on the walls of tombs showing scenes of spinning and weaving. As a state industry, weaving was often supervised by women of the royal harem who were in charge of instructing the textile workers. A charming model of a weaving workshop, found in a tomb of the eleventh dynasty, can be seen in the Egyptian Museum in Cairo.

A dress made from fine woven linen and purported to be the oldest dress in the world [2,800 BC] was donated to the Victoria and Albert Museum and is now on view in their Egyptian room. Even today that dress would not look amiss. The very fine pleating and diaphanous texture remind one of the famous Fortuny textiles. It is sewn with wonderfully tiny whip stitching. There is an abundance of minute stitching, beadwork, sequin decoration, and embroidery on many ancient Egyptian clothes and textiles. How, and with what, was this fine work carried out? Any woman knows that to sew on an every day basis without any finger protection leaves the finger like a pin-cushion. Therefore it seemed worthwhile to examine some of the sewing tools in the Petrie collection of Egyptian excavated artifacts.

The Petrie collection is probably the largest in the world. It has been split mainly between University College London and the museum of Manchester University. It is far more comprehensive than the British Museum, with a fair number of objects directly related to sewing, especially needles. As the needle must precede the thimble, being its reason for existence, attention needs to be given to what kind of needle sewed the fine stitches. There were accounts of short gold needles having been used with fine spun flax thread, but no photos or detailed information appeared in any books on sewing tools that I had read. However, it seemed worth trying to see if there were any in the collection.

Sometimes museums don't have the space to show all the items in their collections, so if you can't find what you want, you have to ask. That was the case with the Petrie collection, but with the help of two very interested and helpful women curators, I found many sewing artifacts. The famous glittering gold needles had been put away in cupboards, due more, perhaps, to guard against loss than to lack of interest. I was very excited at the possibility of actually seeing and touching those legendary fine gold and silver needles that had been used 3000 years BC. Due to the many doubts that had been cast on their existence, it was a moment of vindication when, put away in a drawer, there was the fine silver needle you can see in the photo. Its length is approximately one inch (2.5 cm). The point is sharp and the fine eye is broken halfway up. The silver needle is flanked by a copper pin with a loop head and a large copper needle. All three articles were excavated from the tombs at Naqada from the pre-dynastic period (before 3150 BC).

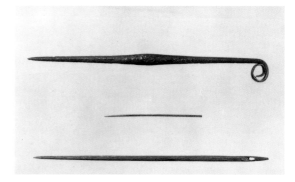

Copper pin, needle in silver, and copper needle found in the Naqada Tombs, pre-dynastic period, before 3000 BC. *Petrie Collection.*

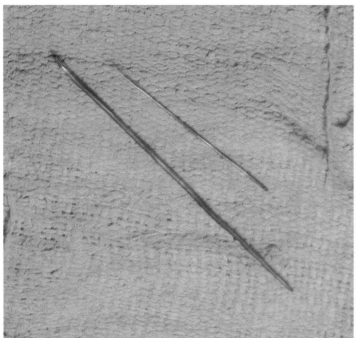

Two fine gold needles from the pre-dynastic period before 2000 BC. *Petrie Collection housed at University College and the University of Manchester.*

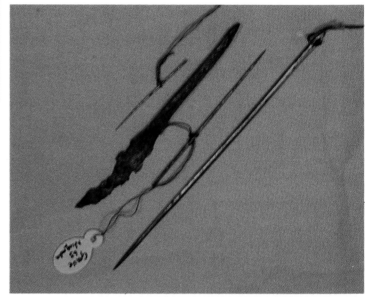

A group of needles and a cutting blade from the pre-dynastic period before 3000 BC, excavated from the tombs of Gizeh and Rifeh. *Petrie Collection.*

The first photo on page 8 shows two gold needles excavated from the tombs at Gizeh and Rifeh dating from some 3000 BC. The larger needle is approximately two inches (5 cm), the smaller approximately one inch (2.5 cm) long. They both have a point at one end and a round eye at the other. Both eyes are intact. Ancient records show that the Egyptians added arsenic to their gold (and silver?) to toughen it, the needles being thus stronger. This adds weight to the possibility of some sort of thimble being in use, as cloth guards would seem liable to be pierced, although it is possible that treated leather might have served. A fair quantity of silver and gold needles have been found, alongside an even larger quantity of needles made from other metals, see photo bottom of page 8.

There is a reasonable possibility that some sewing tools in the Petrie collection may have been overlooked, or not fully understood. In any large museum, vast quantities of untested and unidentified objects remain buried in museum vaults. There are probably as many treasures in their depths as under the earth. In the Petrie collection there are finger rings dating from 5000 BC. These are made in the same expandable fashion as early Chinese sewing rings. Of course many were worn as jewelry, some examples bearing a design of raised punches which look temptingly like thimble dimples. Being convex, their purpose would not have been to hold a needle's point. However, it is not inconceivable that some of the scarab rings made from either steatite, a hard stone covered with glaze, or faience could have been adapted as a form of needle pusher. The design, such as the popular hedgehog complete with indentations to look like quills, could have been used as a pusher in the manner of a tailor's thimble.

Right, Below and Bottom right: Expandable rings. All these expandable rings were probably jewelry and not for sewing. The name "hedgehog design" was the one used by the ancient Egyptians. *Petrie Collection.*

Hedgehog design on a bracelet. *Petrie Collection.*

An expandable ring with raised hedgehog design. *Petrie Collection.*

Clearer view of raised dots in the hedgehog design, on another expandable ring. *Petrie Collection.*

It is not possible to draw any definite conclusions, but I believe a good look through the world of Ancient Egyptian jewelry and textiles might throw up some more sewing items as yet not recognized and correctly identified. Previously flax thread reels had not been correctly labelled, so some sort of needle pusher might still come out of a Pharaoh's tomb. At the moment a leather finger cover seems a possibility, but this would be such a clumsy covering with which to execute such fine stitching. In Japan the finger was often protected by a covering of stiffened material; perhaps this was also the case in ancient Egypt.

Acutrudia, palms, or pushers, used from 11th to 15th centuries, mostly found in Turkey and the Middle East.

China

Ancient China is another civilization which is bound to yield further information. Only this year the tomb of the first Chinese Emperor Qin Shi Huangdi was shown on television, to coincide with the "Mysteries of Ancient China" at the British Museum. Over 2,000 years ago, the Emperor was buried with the bodies of his slaughtered wives (tough being an Empress) along with many artifacts believed to be needed in the celestial worlds. As yet many items remain to be identified. Who knows if a humble sewing tool might roll out from the dust of the Emperor's tomb.

China also produced fine silk thread from 2000 BC onwards, and consequently fine needles must also have existed - though none has survived. However, the earliest thimble yet found is Chinese, taken from the tomb of a minor court official of the Han Dynasty (206 BC - 220 AD). An open top example, it is made of iron (or a type of steel) and was found as part of a complete sewing set.

Trade along the extensive silk routes spread the Chinese knowledge and mastery of steel-working to Asia Minor. The famous Damascus steel industry exported its distinctive Damascene work from c. 200 BC, although as yet no early sewing implements have been found. Bronze acutrudia (held in the palm of the hand to push bodkins or awls through the material being worked) date from c. 100 BC to as late as the seventeenth century, and are early examples of some sort of pushing device.

Gold with cornelian top, found in Carnuntum, in a Roman settlement with other objects dated 2-4th century. As yet we have no conclusive evidence to prove the existence of a Roman thimble.

Example of Acutrudia, some excavated at Ephesus.

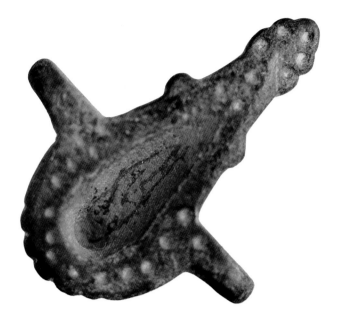

Example of Acutrudia, some excavated at Ephesus.

Example of Acutrudia, some excavated at Ephesus.

Europe

The oldest European thimbles yet discovered were found in the Byzantine sections of Corinth. These thimbles date from the ninth and tenth centuries and are contemporary with the more commonly found earliest Turko-Slavic (Islamic) thimbles made in cast bronze which date from the tenth to the sixteenth centuries. Thimbles have also been found in Cordoba, Spain; these may date from the Moorish occupation of the southern third of Spain from any time between the eighth and fifteenth centuries. Examples of these Hispano-Moresque thimbles can be seen in the archeological museum in Madrid, and they were probably used for heavy work such as carpet-embroidery, saddlery, or sail-making. Small round thimbles have been found in many sites in Asia Minor, and some historians suggest that they may have been brought back by Crusaders and subsequently directly influenced the design of the rounded medieval European thimble.

Open topped thimble very similar to one excavated in Corinth.

An example of a Hispano-Moresque thimble.

By the mid-fourteenth century, plain medieval bronze or brass thimbles, made by casting or hammering, were common in Europe. The acorn-shaped cap that is typical of the time is fairly shallow, and sometimes has a hole in its top (this may have been for ventilation, or may mark the point at which it was held as it was removed from its cast). These medieval thimbles are delicate enough for embroidery. Fine spun thread was by now readily available, although fine needles were costly. During the fifteenth century, brass thimbles continued to be cast in a mold or hammered, but became slightly deeper in shape.

It was the development of the Nuremberg thimble in the early sixteenth century, however, that marked the turning point in European thimble production. In 1530, Nuremberg thimble-makers discovered a superior metal alloy, made of copper and zinc, which created a smooth, bright, brass of an even texture. The Nuremberg craftsmen also produced gold and silver thimbles (as well as fine steel needles) in quantity. These are among the earliest thimbles to be decorated and some bear inscriptions. Makers' marks are sometimes found at the start of the knurled indentations.

In England, fine needle-makers established a factory in Long Crendon, Buckinghamshire, in 1650, and a London needle factory was set up in Threadneedle Street, hence the name. English seventeenth-century thimbles are very distinctive, recognizable by their domed tops, straight sides and tall slim shape. They were made in brass, silver or gold and were often decorated with a form of strapwork. Some bear religious mottoes around the bottom rim, and then indentations appear as square waffles or tiny circles. One of the most important manufacturers of brass working thimbles of the time was John Lofting. He had brought a new casting method with him from Holland in 1693, and was revolutionizing the English thimble-making industry, firstly in his factory in Islington, London, and later at a larger factory in Buckinghamshire. At the end of the seventeenth century, pinchbeck was invented by Christopher Pinchbeck (1670-1732) as an imitation of gold. Some pinchbeck pieces were dipped in gold, i.e. gilded. Pinchbeck thimbles are found in châtelaines of the period.

Eighteenth-century thimbles are more diverse, ranging from squat examples in the early and mid-1700s to straight-sided, round-topped taller versions later in the century. The indentations on thimbles changed from the waffles and circles of the seventeenth century to circles in the early eighteenth century, and to dots (still with us) at the end of the eighteenth century. Meissen started producing porcelain thimbles c. 1720 and squat filigree silver thimbles were also introduced in the early years of the century. Reinforced steel-topped silver thimbles were being produced. Enamelled examples from the English south Staffordshire factories, notably from the area around the town of Bilston, were becoming fashionable.

The elegance of general design prevalent at the end of the eighteenth century was reflected in the work of thimble-makers. Thimbles became taller, and assumed a beehive shape. A popular development at the end of the eighteenth century and the beginning of the nineteenth century was the "toy" thimble containing a tiny scent bottle. Such thimbles were made of gold, silver, ivory or pinchbeck; some examples were mainly decorative in filigree, while others consist of engraved or enamelled decoration on a plain body. The bottle would probably have contained scent or scented oil used to stop fine pins or needles from rusting. The base was attached to the thimble by a screw-on thread inside its rim. The base was additionally engraved with the owner's initials and could be used as a letter seal.

In 1816 the famous Piercy's patent thimble was registered by John Piercy, an English craftsman. His thimbles were made of tortoiseshell embellished with gold and silver, and some featured a shield flanked by a lion and a unicorn. Many versions of this thimble were produced, and on all that I have seen, the shield has been applied crookedly. This does not mean that it has been damaged.

A distinctive wooden thimble of the time is the Tunbridge ware thimble. This sometimes came with its own matching case and was produced by companies such as the George Wise Turnery, c. 1830.

The most famous mother-of-pearl thimbles from the early to mid-nineteenth century came from France. Most were made by artists living and working in the Palais Royal district of Paris and are distinguished by a central oval enamel plaque bearing a pansy or a tiny flower. As the century progressed, the shape of the mother-of-pearl thimbles changed. The beehive shape was typical at the turn of the century, while by 1850 the flat top had become fashionable. Most of the thimbles were made from a single piece of shell and were banded in gilt metal; some bore a tiny gold shield in the middle. Silver thimbles of this period tended to be taller and slimmer with richly decorated borders.

Placing your thimbles in a relevant social and artistic context will often help to date them and trace their origins. It is for this reason that commemorative thimbles are enduringly popular. It is delightful to recreate the scene in your imagination, when, for example, confronted by a thimble celebrating the Great Exhibition at London's Crystal Palace in 1851; you can imagine Queen Victoria perambulating by on the arm of her beloved Albert.

Investigating the needlework current at the time a thimble was made will also improve your understanding of its design and construction. For example, fine work requires fine tools, and it is therefore clear that a large heavy iron thimble of the Byzantine era would not have been used for delicate embroidery of the same date. They must have used something smaller and finer. Many categories of thimble have still to be discovered, as it is apparent that there would always have been a variety of thimbles, each related and suited to needlework of a particular kind.

A Short History of Needlework

The earliest surviving pieces of delicate stitching date from c. 5000 BC and were found in ancient Egyptian tombs. The linen cloth, made from flax, is of fine quality and would have been sewn with fine needles; bodkins (used for holing or threading when working thicker materials) of wood, bone, copper, silver, bronze and gold have also been recovered. Products of the Persian and Babylonian civilizations in existence in c. 3000 BC have also survived. The Babylonians are believed to have invented gold-work around that time using spun gold thread, a technique which the Egyptians were later to develop further.

Fragments of Egyptian tapestry embroidered with fine thread on a linen cloth (now in the Egyptian Museum, Cairo) date from c. 1550 BC and employ some of the Egyptians' favorite design motifs. These included the lotus flower, egg and dart designs, rushes, and the leaves and blossom of the honeysuckle. Expensive gold thread was used for the most prestigious pieces of work, whereas gilded cat gut was employed as a less expensive alternative, for instance in the work decorating Solomon's temple.

By the first century AD, the art of embroidery was so sophisticated that Virgil was moved to describe it as "painting with a needle." From the first to the fourth centuries, Rome produced much embroidery done in purple wool on linen. Indigo was the most expensive dye and purple therefore became the color associated with the Emperors and the aristocracy. The most common motifs in their embroidery were human figures, animals and foliage, particularly trailing vines. By the end of the fifth century, Egypt was exporting embroidery incorporating Christian symbols and scenes from the Gospels. Byzantium, too, was famed for the needlework it was producing during this period.

By the tenth century, Sicily had succeeded Byzantium as a leading center of art and exported the Arabic designs so typical of the pre-Norman period in that region. In England, the art of embroidery flowered between 1250 and 1350, when the Embroiderers' Guild was established, giving rise to a body of work known as the *Opus Anglicanum*. The Syon Cope in the British Museum is a fine example of the standards of the time. A large proportion of the most beautiful English embroidery of this period was designed by monks who otherwise specialized in illuminating manuscripts. The actual sewing was done mainly by women though.

Italian embroidery flourished in the fourteenth century, particularly in Florence. Francesco Squarcione, founder of the Paduan school of painting, was especially renowned for his work in embroidery design. It was common, principally in Italy, for tapestry and embroidery designs ("cartoons") to be produced by painters during this period.

Perhaps the most attractive shaded gold-work ever produced emerged from the rich courts of the Dukes of Burgundy, based in Flanders in the fifteenth century. Known as *or nu* (naked gold), the tradition of rich embroidery work expanded during the following two centuries and influenced fashions at all the European courts. Precious stones and brightly colored intricate designs of flowers and foliage, often using black silk thread on linen, were widely employed on both clothes and domestic items, such as cross-stitch samplers and boxes covered with padded stump-work.

Petit point, the finest form of tapestry, was wide-spread in seventeenth-century France, and by the eighteenth century enormous quantities of needlework were being made throughout Europe, including wall-hangings, clothes, samplers, and silk pictures (landscapes among them). The focus of English embroidery had also become domestic and courtly rather than ecclesiastical, following the reformation and the dissolution of the monasteries. The declining productions and disappearance of many of the skills associated with the sewing of ecclesiastical embroidery were only finally arrested in England in the nineteenth century when the resurgence of the High Church and the consequent demand for greater ecclesiastical ornamentation promoted the revival of decorative embroidery on vestments, pew seats and other church furnishings.

This trend was regrettably reversed again with the invention of the sewing machine, both domestic and commercial, which initiated another decline in embroidery standards. The long-taught skills of domestic needlework, exemplified above all by the delicate and often touching samplers of young girls, have since radically deteriorated.

A brighter note to finish on is today's renewed interest in sewing in its social context. Perhaps the passive isolation provoked by television is being challenged by the ever-growing popularity of quilting, for example in the United States, and lace-making groups in Europe. The lace bobbins, the tatting shuttle, the needle and the thimble are not valued just for the work they are instrumental in, but also for their role in encouraging the binding together of, and the exchange of information between communities. It would be typical, in a small American community in the early nineteenth century for example, for the men to be employed building a grain storing barn, while the women had a sewing and quilting bee. The film "Seven Brides for Seven Brothers" illustrated this well. The difference in an American quilt was that it was padded for warmth, as you might have to survive a bitingly cold winter. These wonderful quilts are still being made and used today. Quilting thimbles are made with concave tops, but are a relatively modern invention. Lace making groups are equally popular now, both in Europe and in the U.S.A.

Chapter 2

Early Medieval and Fifteenth Century Thimbles

The Plantagenets ruled most of England when Henry III succeeded his father John in 1216. London, the south east, and the north of England were ruled by a French king. The French influence was strong in the designs of the period, especially regarding textiles, because King Henry wanted to emulate the greatness of French art. The earliest thimbles that are accessible to the collector now are the small brass acorn tops or skeps, made circa 1350-1400. In general these bear no decoration or markings. At the end of the fifteenth or beginning of the sixteenth century, thimbles with designs such as fleur de lys were being made. The Plantagenets' coat of arms bears two quarterings of the French fleur de lys. It is well to bear that design in mind when we look at some of the early excavated brass thimbles, as the fleur de lys was used on both English and French artifacts.

There is a quantity of these plain fourteenth century thimbles, so it might not be too farfetched to imagine that a great many were used by nuns. Indeed one such thimble was found in a nun's grave of that period. As 1350 was the beginning of the onslaught of the Black Death, which was estimated to have killed off one-third of the population of Western Europe, perhaps these very thimbles played their part in caring for the sick and the orphans. Certainly the first thimbles known to have been used in Britain and Europe date from the fourteenth century. These are sometimes referred to as "skeps" or "acorn tops," and were made mainly from brass. These thimbles are difficult to date with accuracy or confidence; the quality and composition of the metal alloys varied enormously. Even museums are very cautious about metal-testing as a means of establishing a precise date. In addition, if tools are served very well by their shape, this can change very little over time-scales of hundreds of years; the shape of an object therefore is not in itself necessarily a good guide to its date.

Left to right: English medieval; European; English medieval.

The shape of the acorn top is curious because it is so shallow. I have tried several of these little thimbles on, and they just cover the fingertip. The sides are quite wide so they do not grip the finger. The user obviously had no nails. Many of these thimbles have small holes at the top, or at the side, which would have been used to attach them by means of a thong, and possibly served the dual purpose of ventilation. The hole might also have facilitated shedding from the casting.

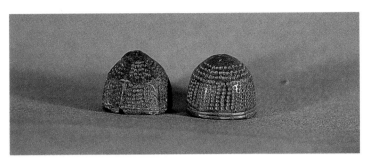

Medieval thimble, c. 1350.

The strong Moorish influence following the Crusades is very evident. Examples of both closed-topped Hispano-Moresque and Turko-Slavic (also known as Islamic or onion top) thimbles, dating from the tenth to the sixteenth centuries, are numerous. The round-topped thimbles excavated from the Levant are rarer.

European medieval thimbles. The center right thimble is an open top.

Until the sixteenth century, metal thimbles were either cast or hammered into a die (mold). Indentations were hand-punched in an orderly fashion, starting from the open end and finishing short of the crown (or top), like a monk's tonsure. The bare crown on the thimble top disappeared with the emergence of the Nuremburg thimbles in the sixteenth century. Some acorn tops show the pleats characteristic of metal thimbles in which the metal cooled too much before it has been adequately hammered.

Makers' marks such as a rowel (spur), dagger, flower, or keys can sometimes be seen at the beginning of the indentations. Unfortunately these remain undocumented, although they are thought to have been introduced c.1530. Apart from an incised line, very little decoration on thimbles is apparent until the sixteenth century.

Early excavated open tops

It is assumed that the ring type (or open top) thimbles must have evolved before the closed top; in fact both shapes had been used for many centuries in tandem, the ring type for heavy work and the closed top for more delicate, intricate embroidery. Although ornamental or decorative thimbles appeared very early in history, both Hispano-Moresque and Turko-Slavic thimbles clearly fall into the heavy working thimble category. It is almost certain that more delicate thimbles for use with finer cloth were made then, but none of these has yet been found.

This thimble has a slightly different onion shape and a decorative border, Hispano-Moresque which shows the Moorish influence.

Hispano-Moresque Thimbles

(see page 20 for more examples)

Hispano-Moresque thimbles have been dated from the twelfth to fifteenth centuries. They were cast in one piece and their distinctive pointed shape bears a close resemblance to the shape of the Moorish soldiers' "helmets." These thimbles have been found in Cordoba, Spain, at a site with other objects of a similar period. One such example is signed in Arabic "made by Al-Sayib."

An ancient Hispano-Moresque example showing the ornamentation at its tip.

An unusual waist-shaped border with interlacing arabesque design.

Fabulous Hispano-Moresque gold thimble excavated in Spain.

Cordoba became renowned for steel-working during the Moor's occupation of southern Spain, from the eighth to the fifteenth centuries. The fine steel needles produced there were extremely costly. Even an affluent woman would rarely have been able to afford more than one at a time.

Hispano-Moresque thimbles have no rims, but some have decorated borders. They are heavy and approximately 2 inches (5 cm) high. The indentations punched around the side stop short of the top and are large and round; this implies that these thimbles were made for use with thick needles and that they were probably used in saddlery or embroidered rug work. Thimbles made in two sections - the cap placed on a cylinder and joined to it with a seam - did not appear until the sixteenth century.

Turko-Slavic Thimbles

(see page 21 for more examples)

The second style of early thimble is known as the Turko-Slavic or onion top thimble. These have been found in Asia Minor across the Balkans to Eastern Europe and are thought to date from as early as the thirteenth century. The typical bulbous top is reminiscent of the domes of mosques and Byzantine churches.

Like the Hispano-Moresque thimbles, they are made of cast bronze and have neat hand-punched indentations stopping short of the top. Some tops are decorated with three or four holes. Border ornaments include turned rings, a small lip or a broad decorated band. These thimbles are generally about 2.5 inches (7 cm) high. Their diameters vary - the larger ones were obviously designed for men and the smaller for women - but they are all very solidly constructed. It has been suggested that the onion-shaped end would originally have been padded inside, making it easier to use; otherwise the tip of the finger had nothing to press against in order to direct the needle. All of the known examples are working thimbles and were probably used for embroidery on rugs, leather, or sewing up bales for transport.

Left, 18th century French; center, Turkish onion shape; right, 16th century European.

Abbasid-Levantine Thimbles

(see pages 22ff for examples)

Abbasid-Levantine thimbles derive their name from their discovery in the Levant, near Baghdad, the center of the Abbasid culture. John von Hoelle (who named them) dates them from the ninth to twelfth centuries, and suggests that they may have been the forerunners of the thimbles we know today, introduced into Europe by the returning Crusaders. Smaller than the Hispano-Moresque and Turko-Slavic thimbles, with a rounder shape and a definite rim, some are decorated with a chevron motif curving from one side of the thimble to the other, or a cross (as on a hot cross bun) on top. A chevron looks like a V, often used to denote a thrusting forward design.

Fine embroidery was certainly being produced in centers of Arabic influence such as Sicily, then ruled by Norman kings, and in the Norman-dominated cities of the Levant. This half-Christian, half-Muslim world enjoyed luxury and refinement, and it seems probable that more delicate thimbles than those discovered to date also existed, both in bronze and, perhaps, in precious metals.

The design motifs on these three main types of thimble show considerable variety. Some Hispano-Moresque thimbles carried small diamond-shaped motifs, and occasionally a curling vine. (The vine motif had been extensively used by Roman designers and reappears in many revivals of the Classical style. It is also a characteristic design on Ameri-

can thimbles of the late nineteenth and early twentieth centuries). Turko-Slavic thimbles are sometimes decorated with geometric motifs around the border and star-shaped motifs or pierced holes on top. The Levantine thimble is the only one of the three to bear a chevron or cross. The chevron had been a popular design in heraldry from the eleventh century onwards, although it appears far earlier as an Egyptian ornament and on the tomb of King Agamemnon in Greece. It might have been inspired by early battle formations of troops.

It is important to remember that in the turbulent Middle Ages, plate (as used in its old sense to mean silver and gold) was one of the most convenient means of securing and storing personal wealth. Household plate was transportable in times of war, and was easily melted down in times of financial crisis. Although plenty of objects were made in plate, relatively few small gold and silver sewing artifacts, made before the middle of the seventeenth century, exist today in their original form. Bronze thimbles have lasted longer and survived intact in greater quantity, primarily because more of them were made, but also because their intrinsic value was very much lower.

Another material widely used in the Middle Ages was *cuir bouilli* (boiled leather). Boiled leather is almost impenetrable and its availability and price would certainly have made it an ideal material from which to make tough thimbles. (Boiled leather was also part of the protective inner wear worn with armor of the era.)

In England the Plantagenets had been superseded by the houses of Lancaster and York. By the end of the fifteenth century the Tudors inherited the English throne. Great displays of wealth and power were used by Henry VII as propaganda to persuade the population of his ability and success. In May 1497 Christopher Columbus had landed in the New World and John Cabot, a Venetian sailor supported and financed by England, landed in America. This was the dawn of the age of adventure and magnificence, of foreign influence on design, especially the revival of the ancient classical worlds of Greece and Rome. At the close of the medieval period, a very different world was emerging.

Early open top.

European medieval thimbles

Extremely early open top, possibly 12th-13th century.

Very unusual straight sided acorn topped style, sometimes called skeps.

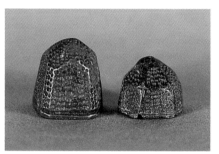

Possibly 13th century

Medieval thimbles. *Courtesy of the British Museum.*

Possibly 13th century open top thimble.

Medieval thimble.

Medieval thimbles.

Another typical example of Hispano-Moresque thimbles, as are those below.

A replica of a 13th or 14th century thimble made by St. Albans Museum and named, in error, "Roman thimble."

These ancient examples show ornamentation at their tips.

Hispano-Moresque Thimbles

(see text on page 17)

All made of brass unless stated. For an interesting example of a brass thimble, $330 plus.

Above and below: Similar thimbles.

Brass thimble found in Spain.

The hole was deliberately placed here, possibly for suspension.

Moorish Influence

(see text on page 17)

Excavated from Turkey and Asia Minor

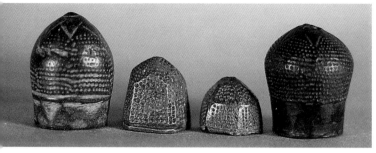

Unusual shape from Asia Minor.

Left: Turkish; center two: English medieval; right: Turkish onion shape.

Typical examples of the period.

Left: Levantine; right three: European.

Four 15th century open tops, possibly for men.

Various European shapes.

Various examples of Moorish influence.

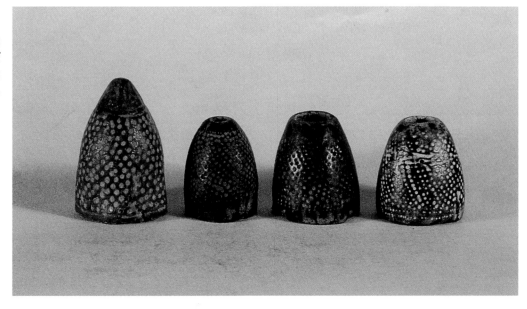

The second and third examples show an European influence.

Levantine shape.

Typical thimble of the period.

Levantine style. Note the crossed over band top.

Chapter 3

Sixteenth-Century Thimbles

Under the Tudors, England ended its long isolation from the continent. Humanism was the logical product of the Renaissance, with the emphasis away from the religious influences of the Medieval period, and towards the classical designs favored by Florence and Rome. The sixteenth century was one of great expansion into new worlds, of explorers, and of flamboyant confidence in the decorative arts. Although the great European ecclesiastical tradition of embroidery had faltered (in England not least because of the Reformation and the dissolution of the monasteries), needleworking skills were turned to more secular and domestic purposes. Gold-thread embroidered clothes, fine linen, wall hangings and rich textiles were all common in the homes of the rich.

In this century appeared one of the most important thimbles ever to have been made. This Elizabethan Renaissance jewel was auctioned by Phillips Midland branch on Dec 13, 1990 and made £18,000 sterling, plus premium. This is the highest price to date to be achieved by a thimble. Asprey's purchased it on behalf of an American collector. The green shagreen case is eighteenth century and therefore not original. The thimble was described as Persian work and Phillips catalog suggested it might have been a present to Queen Elizabeth I (1558-1603) from the Mogul court. The Queen's personal inventory mentions a similar "Persia" needle case.

In construction, the thimble resembled the Indian gold salt cellar at Burghley House, traditionally presented by Queen Elizabeth to Lord Burghley. Of course during the sixteenth century Persia was part of the Indian Empire. If you examine Indian jewelry of that period it is evident that the stone setting was done in the same manner, backing the stones with foil. When the stones were first tested, the description given by Phillips was that they were rubies and paste sapphires set in

An example of a pierced top. The trefoil was an early Arab design, later adopted in Europe.

The Queen Elizabeth I thimble.

This thimble is known as late Levantine. Note the heart motif with arrow through it. There is a strong European influence in the shape.

gold. Asprey's was going to retest the stones as this seemed an odd combination. It is my opinion that stones in that sort of setting often worked loose, and unless you test every stone, some may have been replaced. If you look at the rather squat shape of the thimble it is similar to the early Nuremberg style and to certain sixteenth century excavated thimbles, some with pierced tops. It is also reported in court documents that Elizabeth I of England presented a thimble that had sides richly encrusted with precious stones to one of her ladies-in-waiting; not a very practical object perhaps, but such a gift shows the importance of needlework at the time. The queen herself was a very fine embroiderer. There is a layette that she made for the hoped-for pregnancy of her half-sister, Mary, on view at Leeds Castle.

Silver Thimbles

Until the end of the fifteenth century, German mines had been the main source of silver in Europe, and proximity had therefore encouraged German craftsmen into acquiring exceptional silversmithing skills. However, these mines were almost exhausted by the sixteenth century and Europe increasingly looked for its supplies to the new silver mines being discovered by the Spanish in South and Central America. As a consequence of the greater diversity of sources, silver became more widely available than ever before in a variety of countries, allowing other craftsmen all over Europe to develop their own traditions in silver-working and its associated arts.

Silver thimbles were subsequently made by two types of craftsmen: silversmiths who wished to add a new item to their range of wares or who had received a special commission; and specialist thimble-makers who wanted to apply their existing metal-working skills to a new medium.

Engraved Lettering

A very useful dating device is noting the manner of any engraved lettering. According to *English Engraved Silver* by Charles Oman, the earliest black letter (double outline lettering) engraving appeared at the end of the fourteenth century. From that point inscriptions are plentiful down to the Renaissance. Capital letters were not used as this would spoil the design. In the fifteenth century it became usual to have a capital letter at the beginning of any inscriptions. Black letter inscriptions continued in use until the first quarter of the sixteenth century, but by the end were competing with Roman capitals. By the middle of the sixteenth century sinuous interlacing, often trailing vine, appeared as a typical Renaissance design. Alongside the classically inspired designs were the Moorish influences seen in the rather more formal arabesques of floral scrolls in panels of interlacing strap-work. The end of the sixteenth century showed a great interest in floral motifs and botanical designs. Any inscriptions at all were executed in crude Roman capitals, practically scratched on. This was partly to avoid being accused of Popery and its use of religious Latin inscriptions, executed in elegant Gothic script.

Left: a pierced top thimble; right: a tailor's ring. *Courtesy of the British Museum.*

Note the snake like pattern.

A fine example of a silver thimble made by a silversmith at this time is on view at the Metropolitan Museum of Art in New York. It consists of two parts, has a Renaissance design of racing hounds and is dated 1577. One of the most renowned craftsmen to make and design thimbles was the German John Theo de Bry, who worked in Frankfurt between 1528 and 1598, as a designer for metal engravers. Some of his work (though none of his thimbles, as none has been found) can be seen on knife handles; prints of his designs are kept in the Victoria and Albert Museum Print Room in London.

The thimble designs of de Bry, which, alas, do not seem to have been produced, as none have been identified. *Courtesy of the Victoria and Albert Museum.*

Early silver thimbles were not produced purely for decoration or ornament. In fact, silver is an eminently sensible metal with which to make thimbles because it does not mark the thread (as a base metal can) and, unlike brass, will not aggravate an infection in a cut or pin-prick.

The first filigree thimbles (an outer sleeve of filigree being applied over a smooth inner body)

appeared in the sixteenth century, as did the early examples of toy (in its original sense of meaning miniature trinket) thimbles. These date mostly from the end of the century and were intended as delightful gifts rather than as practical sewing accessories. They were made of two parts, with a removable cap; a shield concealed inside the cap bore the date of manufacture and the owner's initials carved under crystal. Their sides were decorated with formal medallions, quatrefoils and scrolls.

Nuremberg Thimbles

The most important of all thimble-making centers at this time was to be found in Nuremberg. The craftsmen there had been well established in the fifteenth century but it was not until the middle and late sixteenth century that they really grew to dominate the industry. They made base and precious metal (silver) thimbles. Their success was founded on two inventions: the discovery of a better "recipe" for brass and a technique that allowed them to make thimbles from two parts. They were able to apply patterns to flat sheets of metal which were then rolled up and cut into cylinders; the caps were soldered on. The technological developments in founding (the process of making sheets of metal of uniform thickness, color and consistent quality) made in the first quarter of the sixteenth century, permitted by the more efficacious combinations of copper and other metals, in c.1530 facilitated the production of a beautiful, light, bright, almost gold-like brass, which was both popular and easier to work.

All early Nuremberg thimbles. They are well made, with fine regular dimpling.

The significance of the production of consistent high-quality sheet metal is hard to over-estimate. In 1537 specialist sheet metal thimble-makers broke away from the Coppersmiths Guild to form their own guild.

European metal thimbles up to this time had been manufactured in two ways: by the simplest of all metal-working techniques-the alternate heating and hammering (annealing) of thin sheets of metal into shape; and by casting (pouring molten metal into molds). The earliest thimble-making method of all had been simply to hammer thimbles into molds. The thimbles so made are, not surprisingly, very crude compared to the work of the Nuremberg thimble-makers.

This thimble is probably an early Nuremberg product. Note the pointed top, the lack of rims, and fine metal which feels sharp.

The thinner, more regular sheets of metal at the disposal of the Nuremberg craftsmen allowed them greater scope for design and decoration; taller, more elegant shapes and more intricate ornamentation became the order of the day. In the case of single-part thimbles, the basic shapes were first created from discs cut out of the thin sheet metal, heated, then punched into molds. Additional patterns and knurlings were then finished by hand with finer

tools, and the whole would finally be cleaned with acid and polished to a bright sheen. Two-part thimbles were cut out in exactly the same way, with smaller discs being cut for the tops. The construction of these thimbles alone is therefore of little or no value in dating them. The Nuremberg thimble is, however, very distinctive. A typical specimen has a flattish top and a tall slim body, widening towards the base. The brass used looks like matt gold, with a light, delicate feel to it and hand-punched indentations. These indentations form a spiral, winding up the sides and continuing over the thimble's top, their fineness a sure sign that they were used with finer needles. A maker's mark - such as a clover leaf - sometimes appears at the base of the spiral. Such marks are of interest, but cannot, unfortunately, be traced to individual makers. Nuremberg thimbles frequently have a decorated border of rows of small round medallions containing crosses (of Byzantine origin) around their rim. Very similar designs characterize lace ruffs of the period. The shorter, stubbier style of Nuremberg thimble, often made in two parts, had a pointed top or cap.

Various types of metal were employed in early thimble-making. They principally fall into the categories of pure copper, brass (an alloy of copper and zinc), and bronze (an alloy of copper and tin). Metal-working, and consequently thimble-making, skills naturally tended to concentrate around the areas in which the metals were mined, and a special expertise was developed in Germany and Scandinavia (particularly Sweden), and parts of Spain.

The great European age of the Renaissance was coming to a close. The love of grace and freedom in the arts was still evident, but declining. Elizabethan England remained brilliant to the last. There was a great flowering of all the arts under her patronage. The reign of the house of Tudor ended with Elizabeth's death on March 24, 1603, and a new dynasty, the House of Stuart, came to the throne.

Thimbles excavated in Europe. Left: fleur de lys design; right three: similar designs.

Good example of an early maker's mark.

Two thimble tops marked with a cross drawn in a Celtic manner.

Nuremberg thimble with Renaissance influenced design.

Thimbles excavated in Europe with the fleur de lys design.

Nuremberg. The design may be Byzantine.

Another unusual top

More Nuremberg thimbles.

A top showing a similar design to those found on crotal bells. It is believed that the metal works that produced the bells, used on the necks of beasts, also made thimbles. *Courtesy of the British Museum.*

Two open topped versions. *Courtesy of the British Museum.*

Chapter 4

Seventeenth-Century Thimbles

The seventeenth century in Europe was a period of turmoil, unceasing warfare, and strife, but also one of artistic genius. Religious persecution was rampant and caused huge numbers of European artisans to leave their homes and seek refuge in foreign countries where they could live and work in peace. This meant an exchange of skills and ideas in the worlds of fine and decorative arts such as had never been seen before.

The Civil War in England had a marked effect on all the crafts and arts, including thimble-making. Whereas before the Civil War, silver had been widely used - albeit often gilded - in thimbles and other household items, it suffered the same fate as other metals and was frequently melted down to provide material for weapons, armor, and helmets, or to raise money. Most pieces that survived are remarkable for their sloppy workmanship, clumsy construction and relatively plain appearance. Warfare, not the domestic life, was paramount.

Brass, typical strapwork design made in the common two pieces of cap and cylinder.

Very rare leather thimble with square and dot design.

Early 17th century thimbles. *Courtesy of the British Museum.*

In Holland, however, Protestantism in no way cramped decorative styles. Holland's decisive victory against its Spanish enemies brought independence by the middle of the century, and with it peace and financial prosperity. Relative economic stability prevailed again after the war with England and the Civil War, and fostered further technological advances. Less is known of thimble-making in Holland than in Germany, mainly because the industry was not so concentrated in individual towns and cities.

Thimble history was made when John Lofting, a Dutch entrepreneur, moved to England in 1688, bringing with him his new technique of brass casting. He had Anglicized his name to John Lofting, and, after an initial failed venture involving patent fire engines, concentrated his attention on thimble-making. He set up a factory in Islington, London, and his breakthrough came in 1693 when he obtained a patent (Number 319) for a new casting method, previously unused in England. He later moved to Great Marlow, Buckinghamshire, where his factory, eventually powered by a water-mill, was able to turn out well over 150,000 thimbles a month.

One of the famous 17th century brass thimbles made by John Lofting who left Holland and set up his factory in England. Note the typical flat bands top and bottom, $3,200.

Lofting soon dominated the market, his success built on three elements. First was his personal technical knowledge of and expertise in brass casting and knurling by machine. Second was his great entrepreneurial flair, especially in stealing the burgeoning American market from his Dutch rivals. Third was his insistence on quality. His thimbles are noticeably better finished than those of his competitors, and are more comfortable to use. His factory continued to trade successfully well into the eighteenth century. Lofting died in 1742.

Mid-seventeenth century English thimbles tended to be rather crude and rudimentary, both in workmanship and design. Most thimbles had no rim, but were simply finished with one or two incised lines. They were tall and cylindrical, and were usually made in two parts. Often when they are excavated, the join at the side is very visible. This is because the seventeenth century soldering has dissolved. In order to stop the gap widening, a strong glue down the crack can be used to prevent further deterioration. The knurlings or punches were always in patterns of waffles or small circles. Strapwork ornamentation was often used in the form of a chevron or in a "Z" down the thimble's side.

The motto reads 'God is Love.'

Clock-dial tops were also used. Mottoes were often engraved around the thimble's base, usually exhorting the user to industry ("Soe not sleeping") or alluding to the transitory nature of life. A thimble bearing the legend "Live to die" must have been a rather depressing companion for a quiet evening's needlework.

Reverse of the previous thimble. Religious mottoes were famous at this period due to Puritan influence.

Two 17th century silver thimbles. The one on the left shows the typical strapwork design of the mid-17th century. *Courtesy of the British Museum.*

"Matting" ornamentation made its first appearance at this time and has been in continuous use on thimbles ever since. It was originally applied to the base of tankards and candlesticks, and comprises a series of thin engraved bands arranged to form a simple border.

Examples of late 17th century thimbles. All $480 up.

Towards the end of the century, a rounder, shorter thimble shape became fashionable, and the waffle motif gave way to circular patterns. Moral and religious mottoes began to disappear, but domestic platitudes remained popular, and there was a vogue for thimbles bearing their owner's initials. The Rhode Island Historical Society possesses three mid-seventeenth century thimbles, one of which is a sewing ring bearing an engraved heart and inscribed "Esther Willit - 1660-1665." The earliest commemorative thimble, celebrating the marriage of Charles II to Catherine of Braganza in 1662, which can be seen in the Museum of London, is an equally fascinating contemporary piece. The rope twist was being used as a border motif. An even rarer commemorative depicting Charles II on one side and the Boscobel Oak on the reverse, was sold at Christies in may 1995.

Towards the end of the century there was an increasing vogue for floral designs of a mock botanical nature. The subjects are often tulips and irises, engraved in a flowing and somewhat fantastical manner. This type of engraving can be seen on some sewing compendiums rather than on single thimbles. The engraving is always of a sinuous nature, and very linear. By the close of the Caroline period engravers had recovered their lost confidence caused by the Puritan influence, but lettering, such as initials, was still rather primitive and undistinguished. The engraved hearts that often enclose initials have rather sharp points, and sometimes straight sides in the manner of a triangle. Queen Anne was the last Stuart to rule Britain, reassuringly English and ordinary after the dark foreign charms of the previous Stuarts. As she had no heir, the Protestant House of Hanover was invited to take the throne.

Rare filigree thimbles. The one on the left has an inner sleeve of low carat gold.

Brass thimbles of this period will be from $325 upwards and silver examples from $1000, always dependent on design and condition.

A strapwork design mid-17th century brass thimble.

Squashed due to excavation, late 17th or very early 18th century thimble, possibly Dutch.

Very rare curved interlacing strapwork and petalled top in brass, damaged when found.

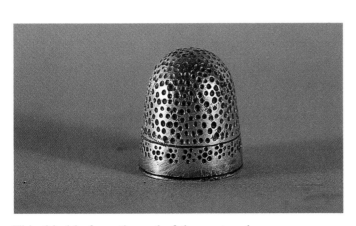

This thimble from the end of the century has a more rounded shape.

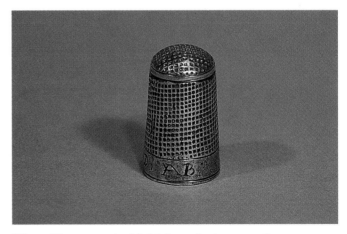

Silver. Note scratched initials at the bottom; there were no elegant inscriptions at this period.

Typical strapwork. The motto reads "Ever True."

Another end of the century thimble. Note the two hearts and the two cherubs. We have left the religious influence and are moving towards the secular.

This textile sample shows the same Arab influence strapwork design found on the thimbles.

Very rare filigree needle and thimble holder.

Silver thimble, probably Dutch.

Silver thimble, c. 1770. Note the different shape. The motto reads "Do Not Lose Me."

Reverse of the previous piece, showing rather naïve portrait engraving.

End of the 17th century group of silver thimbles.

Unusual mid-17th century design.

Note the makers initials at the side: NO.

Mixed group of silver thimbles.

The rounded dimples appeared at the end of the 17th century. Here you can see the construction of the thimble with the central join.

Left: Note rare central open-topped thimble with border of greyhounds, probably Dutch.

Chapter 5

Eighteenth-Century Thimbles

The eighteenth century was known throughout the Western world as The Age of Enlightenment. A prominent theme of Enlightenment thought was the view that people are capable of infinite improvement. After the ravages of the Wars of Religion, improvement was sought through reason and tolerance, and was pursued with verve. Britain was united under the Georges, nationalism was frowned upon, and there was a genuine desire to live according to a benevolent order stemming from principles contained in the nature of mankind and society. That seeking for a natural order, harmony, and balance is evoked in the architecture and general design of the period, demonstrated artistically with great vitality, and practically in the improved practices of production.

By the end of the seventeenth century, the Dutch thimble industry was beginning to lose its business to English and German competitors. There were at least five German factories in the valley of the river Lenne, in south Westphalia, the most notable of which was owned by Johan Casper Rumpe. Rumpe enjoyed the patronage of Frederick the Great, who perhaps more than any other monarch, sought to create a modern Prussia by using scientific methods. Rumpe's basic method of production was casting and then hand-finishing and his company specialized in inexpensive well-made metal thimbles; they are still in production today.

England had its own prospering brass trade by then and no longer needed to import thimbles from overseas. John Lofting's mill continued production into the eighteenth century. Finds of his brass thimbles in the United States, England, and the Netherlands suggest that they were in great demand. The shape of his thimbles is very distinctive; the top looks like a cap placed atop an encircling flat band. The dimpling was finer and more even than comparable thimbles of the time. Birmingham had a flourishing trade in small brass toys (in the sense of trinkets), such as thimbles, buckles and buttons, alongside that of its silverware. Joseph Ashwell and Walter Davenport were registered there in the trade directory of 1769 as thimble-makers.

The same year saw the patenting of an important invention for applying metal ornamentation, John Ford's patent Number 935. Raised patterns were formed on a sheet of metal which was pressed by machine between two dyes (stamps), one dye being convex and the other concave, rather like placing one jelly mold inside another. This gave far greater scope for design on less expensive goods and effectively foreshadowed the end of the hand-crafted metal thimble. After a period of experimentation, mass-production of metal thimbles became a reality. Of course this made thimbles more accessible to everyone, but mass-production often causes a drop in individual designs.

The collector's interest in base metal thimbles is obviously not connected solely with the value of the materials from which they are made or with aesthetic considerations, but with their craftsmanship, antiquity, historical associations and so on. The mass-production of thimbles therefore often renders them less interesting to

Undecorated early 18th century silver thimble.

the collector. It is amusing to think that the rare thimbles we seek today owe their very rarity to the fact that the design did not catch on at the time, so there were fewer made.

The eighteenth century saw a general diminution in the power of the monarchy and a corresponding increase in the power of elected government. Queen Anne reigned from 1702 to 1714, followed by George I, II, and III, up to 1820. The elected government curbed the monarch's ambitions, while encouraging greater national prosperity. New industrial methods accelerated the number and range of everyday and luxury goods produced and more people could afford them. The eighteenth century fashion for trifles, *objets de vertu, vitrine* and *galenterie* (including thimbles) which originated in France, took Europe by storm. Silver sewing compendiums, thimbles containing scent bottles and 18ct gold sets are good examples.

Rare French gold thimble with enamelled border, gold lettering reads "Profitez du Temps." Shown with its case.

Three main thimble shapes succeeded each other as the century progressed. Needleworkers in the first half of the century preferred the shorter rounder shape, which then declined in popularity in favor of a return to the tall, slim thimble with a rounded top. The last of the three, the beehive form, appeared towards the end of the century. Until the 1750s or so, thimbles were still being made in two pieces - a top and a cylinder. A gentle widening of the base in relation to the top as the century progressed was accompanied by the addition of a border which often carried decoration (in lieu of a rim). Indentations were small and round, retaining the circular look prevalent at the end of the previous century and the waffle indentations on the sides of

the thimbles had ceased. Occasionally tiny dots were used in between the circular indentations. The thimble tops had both round and waffle-shaped indentations, but rarely any rims.

In the second half of the century, metal thimbles began to be made in one piece using a technique known as the "deep drawn" method. "Deep drawing" shapes the thimble from a small, flat, round disc which is hammered into a dye or mold. This method of production was largely responsible for pushing the trend towards taller, slimmer thimbles, which needed in some cases to be reinforced with the introduction of steel tops. Beehive thimbles were made in one piece, with indentations reaching down to the border at their base. The reason for the more costly thimble to be made with a taller top was to allow for a longer finger nail belonging to an aristocratic lady.

Neo-classical border on a mid-18th century silver thimble.

Thimble decoration certainly changed to suit current tastes (the Neo-classical design favored by Robert Adam and Rococo styles), but not so drastically that working thimbles lost their primarily functional raison d'etre. The more restrained Neo-classical style prevailed on decorative thimbles that had still to retain their full function; more extravagant Rococo designs were favored for elaborate châtelaines and étuis, prized for their fine workmanship and expensive materials more than for their utility. Exceptional workmanship is evident in certain Rococo gold and tortoiseshell thimbles cases and in gold thimbles. The typically wavy, almost waisted outline on some thimble containers, the chasing of tiny flowers and leaves, and even the use of a natural material such as shell in luxurious harmony with gold are all classic examples of the Rococo style at its finest.

Very rare 18 ct gold and tortoiseshell rococo style thimble holder and matching gold thimble.

Imagine elegant court ladies, sitting after dinner, chatting and sewing. The flashing little gold thimble must have brought admiration and status to the owner. When my mother was asked by a fellow collector why French sewing tools were often finer and more luxurious than British ones, she replied that she wasn't sure whether that was because French husbands were more generous, or if they had guiltier consciences!

Thimbles as Toys

(see pagse 49ff for more examples)

Decorative thimbles and other "toys" were also being introduced alongside practical working thimbles. Silver compendiums, mainly made in England, Germany, and Italy are particularly interesting: a compendium unscrews to reveal a thimble, a letter powderer, a needle-holder and a letter seal. Sometimes if you undo and look at each piece carefully, you will see numbers scratched on the surfaces. I believe this was done to facilitate assembly. Ribbon-like interlacing and chasing in Moorish patterns recurs frequently as a design. Filigree (wire-work) was a very popular technique used in the creation of sewing toys, and all manner of small objects such as boxes, marriage caskets, bodkin cases and many others.

Other variations included thimbles with a tape measure or a pin-cushion. Some had a fingerguard that screwed onto a base containing a tiny emery cushion; the guard was then covered by a thimble, but it is sadly now almost always missing. The bases of these toys often had engraved initials and are thought to have been used to seal letters. Most of the toys that have survived are in silver, gold or pinchbeck and command very high prices. These scent bottle combinations continued into the 19th century.

Above: Silver filigree combination toy of tape measure and thimble unscrewing to reveal miniature scent bottle.

A further variety of silver filigree thimbles and toys.

This gives you an idea of how these compendiums unscrew. $2500.

A Short History of Filigree

Filigree was particularly popular in England towards the end of the seventeenth century, following the marriage of Charles II to the Portuguese Catherine of Braganza in 1662. Bombay, which is Portuguese for the Good Bay, was part of her dowry, and filigree work originally came from India. First fairly large caskets came over, then, owing to their popularity, silversmiths from India arrived and set up workshops, until eventually the technique became incorporated in the manufacture of English everyday objects. Certainly thimbles, bodkin cases, and thimble cases were made in the seventeenth century, but many more remain from the late eighteenth century. Italian silversmiths also excelled in the technique, and the largest settlement of Italians was registered in Clerkenwell in the 1780s. In fact amongst many collectors, the name Clerkenwell Work is used for eighteenth century filigree.

18th century silver filigree with flat top.

Filigree thimble. $480.

The stubbier 18th century version of a silver filigree.

Another silver filigree thimble. These were immensely popular, although one would imagine them to be impractical.

As a guide to dating a piece of filigree, the following details of construction might help. The 1680 pieces have heavier "skeletons." The main ribs are slightly thicker, made from one mill square section wire. This is filled in with the typical tiny wire scrolls, made from two fine wires twisted together. The scrolls or circles only go approximately once round. In England the hinges, for example on a box or thimble case, were always made from heavier, plain silver. The whole item has a slightly firmer, heavier, and more symmetrical look than the eighteenth century pieces. In contrast, on mid-seventeenth century articles from the continent, for example Holland, the hinges

Rare 17th century filigree thimble with the detail of top.

were made from twisted silver wire, not heavier, plain silver. The reason for this was that the general silver gauge was thinner, therefore you did not have the weight needed to solder.

In the eighteenth century, the filigree "skeleton" was lighter. The secondary "loops" are often longer. These loop shapes are the same as those found on

Paisley shawls, also originating in India, symbolizing the seed of life. The loops are in turn filled with tiny scrolls or circles, which by now are much tighter, going round three times. This sort of work is typically found on the taller slimmer thimbles and thimble toys containing scent bottles. The squatter shaped thimbles are either seventeenth century, or early- to mid-eighteenth. They are harder to date accurately, being small and, probably not being a fashionable object, subject to less marked changes. The nineteenth century filigree is often even tighter and thinner in look, with less marked changes between the skeleton and the in-fill wire circles.

Interestingly, some stubbier filigree thimbles have a kind of inner sleeve. I thought one that I possessed looked tarnished, only to find that the inner sleeve was a low carat gold, under an outer silver filigree top. My thimble was thought by a filigree expert to be seventeenth century, so you can see it in the seventeenth century chapter. Various combinations were used in making later thimble toys, the most famous being a thimble screwing onto a base containing a miniature scent bottle as first seen in the preceding century. The scent bottle can be clear or blue glass. Do not be tempted, as was a friend of mine, to clean out the white sediment at the base of the bottle. This is the remainder of the original plaster of Paris used to keep the bottle in place.

There is a very fine collection of filigree objects at Chatsworth in Derbyshire, home of the Duke and Duchess of Devonshire.

Eighteenth Century Porcelain

These thimbles are highly sought after. The vital factor affecting their value is the quality of the painting. They have the added charm of being very colorful, combined with an air of fragile delicacy. Their fragility is also the cause of their rarity. Certainly fine porcelain has always kept pace with, and often superseded, the price of silver and gold.

The eighteenth century was the great age of porcelain, a fine ceramic ware, white, translucent and very delicate. It was first developed and exploited in China and was named after its country of origin, although the English word porcelain comes from the Italian *porcellana* as in little pig. Unfortunately, very few porcelain thimbles of the period exist, and many of those that have come down to us are difficult to attribute with any certainty. Because of this, accredited eighteenth-century porcelain thimbles are highly sought after and consequently fetch very high prices at auction.

Meissen

One of the first documented porcelain thimbles is recorded in the list of the great Meissen factory (the first to manufacture "hard paste" porcelain in Europe) in Germany in the early 1700s, under the category *Gallanterien*, which can be translated in this context as "fancy goods." There is little pretence that these porcelain thimbles were ever intended for practical work. They were fashioned purely as decorative objects - as beautiful gifts and keepsakes for wives and sweethearts - and for this reason they have a very special place in the romance of thimble-collecting. (China thimbles do, however, have a specific use in needlework, as their smooth texture makes then ideal for working with silk). A collector came to see me, wanting a wedding present for her daughter, whose name was Sarah. On my glass shelf was a delicate white, fine porcelain thimble. It was banded top and bottom with gold, and decorated in flowing gold script with one word, Sarah, a case of serendipity.

Above four: The minutely painted scene all around the border is an example of why Meissen artisans are considered the finest porcelain painters in the world. Nearly all their thimbles fetch over $8400.

Another variety of a Meissen thimble with a fine mono-chrome design, and the initials JE.

A tiny scene around the border with an unusual red top.

This variety has a painting within a cartouche. Most of these thimbles show the Meissen mark of crossed swords inside.

Because most Meissen thimbles now exist in private collections, it is very difficult to calculate how many actually survive, but it would be a great surprise, given what we know, if there are more than about 500 - of which only a handful are in public collections and museums. At probably the most important auction of thimbles ever held, at Christie's Geneva showrooms in 1975, no less than 103 Meissen thimbles went under the hammer, all of which were fully authenticated, and many of which were, in addition, accredited to individual artisans and painters. A world record price of 21,000 Swiss francs was paid for a continuous seascape thimble featuring off-shore ships, attributed to Ignaz Preissler at Breslau. This record price was broken in 1979, when Christie's auctioned 10 Meissen thimbles, among them a small thimble from the 1740s depicting a harbor scene, which sold for a hammer price of £8000. Recently, in 1995, Meissen thimbles were fetching an average of £6000, depending on the painting.

Landscapes and seascapes are popular Meissen subjects, as are people fishing or hunting, and birds and flowers depicted in oriental style. Many Meissen thimbles have a distinctive rounded form, but the Cummer Gallery of Art in Jacksonville, Florida, has a collection of eight eighteenth-century Meissen thimbles, the shapes of which vary considerably. One has a waisted effect, tied around with a painted blue bow on a plain white background and with a gilded interior; another is very small and squat, with two plain yellow bands at top and bottom; and a third has a flat top, is tall and slim, and is painted all over with many-colored "Deutsche-Blumen" flowers. This Deutsche-Blumen pattern was introduced c.1735, inspired by Chinese and Japanese work. It shows stylized oriental flowers outlined in a darker color.

The trademark of Meissen consists of two crossed swords, painted in underglaze blue, but this is not always present. Meissen thimbles can usually be readily identified by the painting style, which is always fine, and shows meticulous attention to detail: gilding inside the thimble is also a good indica-

tor, but again, this is not always found.

Meissen designs were heavily influenced by Chinese and Japanese decoration found on the costly items regularly imported to Europe from the Far East at that time. Because of their great commercial success, and the facility with which they reinterpreted oriental hard paste porcelain, most of their contemporary European rivals copied Meissen, although there is not here, as there is in other thimble categories, much danger of confusion in attribution. These competitors and imitators included factories at Furstenberg, Ludwigburg, Nymphenburg and possibly Hochst, in Germany; Schooren in Switzerland; and Du Paquier in Vienna, but documentation is incomplete and, in any case, none of their production can be said to rival Meissen either in artistry or scale of output.

Elsewhere in Europe, the Royal Copenhagen factory in Denmark certainly produced some porcelain thimbles, but they lacked the refined elegance of the Meissen peers. Thimbles were also manufactured at the Royal Factory in Naples, Italy, of which a small number still exist, and in Mennecy-Villeroy, in France. However, it is only in England that any genuine attempt was made to compete with Meissen, certainly in quantity, if seldom in design. It is ironic that the growth of the market for porcelain thimbles in England came at a time when the Meissen factory had all but ceased production.

Generally, records for the earliest part of the eighteenth century are vague, and though thimbles other than Meissen have come down to us, attribution is difficult and most uncertain. Factory documentation shows that porcelain thimbles were being

18th century Chelsea porcelain. Note the French inscription.

manufactured in quantity, yet relatively few examples exist. This may be due to their fragility, or to the fact that they were damaged easily, and so were discarded.

In England in the late eighteenth century, the Chelsea factory and the Worcester Porcelain Company (previously named Chamberlain Worcester) all included soft paste thimbles in their list of wares. It was not until the nineteenth century that the fashion really took hold, and the market was then quickly dominated by Worcester.

Porcelain had become a standard product by the end of the eighteenth century. When Chamberlain (later to become Chamberlain Worcester) commenced manufacture in 1790, there were fewer than 10 porcelain producers in the British Isles, but by the 1840s-50s there were nearly 100. One of the earliest pieces of evidence of porcelain thimble manufacture in England is a thimble waster, or mould, found in one of the store rooms of the Worcester Porcelain Company dating from c.1785. The 1795 Christmas stock-taking at Chamberlain recorded 300 unglazed thimbles for sale at one penny each, and an order page dated January 1, 1796 shows a stock of 25 dozen Worcester thimbles, with a further 66 in the Chamberlain shop, proving that significant thimble production existed at that time. There is some evidence of a limited production of Derby porcelain thimbles; in the list of molds, one entry in 1795 refers to "eight thimbles."

Many of the soft paste thimbles produced by the Chelsea factory bear French mottoes such as, "Gage de mon amitié," which is found on one example in the Victoria and Albert Museum. Since the fashion for toy thimbles came from France, British manufacturers would regularly add French inscriptions to their pieces. This would be in the same manner of giving designs French sounding names to add glamor to Madame's toilette.

Silver Thimbles

The more expensive English thimbles of this period were not made exclusively of porcelain however. Aside from purely functional, practical

thimbles in base metals, very fine examples continued to be made in gold or silver.

A silver thimble with typical graceful neo-classical border and a steel top.

A similar border, but without the steel top. $800.

Two silver thimbles with steel tops made by the famous woman silversmith, Hester Bateman. The initials H and B intertwine in the border design. $1600.

One of the earliest silversmiths whom it is possible to name is Hester Bateman, who inherited the business on her husband's death. The expertise in management and good taste in design that she exhibited enabled her business to flourish in

London. Objects produced between 1761-1790 included excellent working thimbles in a controlled Neo-classical style. If the border of a Bateman thimble is closely examined, the initials "HB" will be found chased into the pattern, rather than stamped on with the customary silver punch: this may have been a means of avoiding assay office costs on these small items. Many Hester Bateman thimbles are steel-topped.

London was not the only place in England producing high-quality silverware. The rise of Birmingham as a manufacturing city producing silver objects of significance first became evident in the latter half of the seventeenth century, and its position was finally assured when Matthew Bolton, a silversmith and businessman, managed to obtain permission to open an assay office there in 1773. Before this, all goods had to be sent to London for taxing, which could often result in delay, and sometimes in theft and damage. Important manufacturers such as Matthew Linwood, Matthew Arnold, and Samuel Pemberton all founded substantial silver-working companies in the area, each of which maintained a large output of thimbles. It must be said that Samuel Pemberton is more famous for his superbly decorated, bright cut needle cases. The initials S.P. are often to be found stamped at one end. The date letter and assay mark are not always included, but this is no reason to doubt their authenticity. Bright cut engraving first appeared circa 1775, the sparkling reflection making it immensely popular. The fashion continued into the nineteenth century.

American Thimbles

In the United States, there is very little evidence of early porcelain thimble manufacture, and although there was a limited production of silver and base metal thimbles, many of the silver thimbles used until the eighteenth century were imported. This may not be popular with American collectors, but generally designs of this period were approximately twenty years behind those in Europe. The chief centers of silversmithing during the period of settlement [seventeenth century] were the port towns of Boston and New York. Boston was largely inhabited by English settlers. Daniel Neal, in his "History of New England" 1720, estimated the value taken from England by 1670 to the four New England settlements at some £500,000, going towards a quarter of the British nation's wealth.

In a will of Antipas Boyse 1669, along with an inventory of many silver items, there is mention of "9 buttons for breeches, thimble," etc. Three generations of craftsmen, the Richardsons, are known to have worked in Philadelphia from 1681 onwards into the eighteenth century, and there are records of Joseph Richardson, silversmith, topping silver thimbles with steel. Although English silversmiths concentrated on making the newly-fashionable tall, slim thimbles as the century progressed, American craftsmen retained their preference for a shorter, stubbier style: indeed, American thimbles look noticeably shorter than European thimbles throughout the eighteenth, nineteenth, and early twentieth centuries. Did American women keep their nails shorter than their European sisters? Or were U.S.A. silversmiths more frugal in their use of materials and changing technology?

Although some records exist of thimbles being included alongside other items, it is not until the 1760s that there is evidence of anyone claiming to specialize solely in thimble manufacture. Probably the first American to promote himself exclusively as a thimble-maker was one Benjamin Halstead, of New York and Philadelphia - in fact he was confident enough to advertise in 1794 that his production was now large enough to supply the whole United States, and that citizens should therefore boycott lower-quality imported thimbles. His business flourished - though his claims about the superiority of his products over the imported thimbles were highly tenuous - and there is evidence that his son opened a separate manufacturing unit on Varick Street, New York, *c.* 1814.

Victory in the Seven Years War had given Britain mastery of the oceans and provided the financial impetus for the Industrial Revolution, enabling Britain to become a great exporter of goods the world over. America had been born as a new nation, encompassing the new ideals of democracy, and started to discover an American identity in manufacture and design. At the turn of the century, Europe was beginning to be dominated by Napoleon, so French designs in all things, including thimbles and sewing tools, were considered the apogee of elegance. "Made in Paris" was embossed on the fine sewing sets that most elegant women wanted to display. In a delightful book *The Memoires of the Duchess d'Abrantes* written at the court of Napoleon by a friend of Josephine's, the Duchess describes the delicious little sewing tools, including a thimble, presented to a young lady in her *Corbeille de Marriage*. This was a marriage basket containing useful objects needed for the bride's trousseau. During the ceremony, the Duchess comments on the Empress Josephine's elegant attire, adding casually "such a pity she has no teeth."

Enamel Thimbles

The eighteenth century also saw the serious development of thimbles in enamel. The word is derived from the French *amail* or *esmail* and enamel itself is made from a mixture of silica, minium and potash, which, when it is in its molten state, is colored with various chemicals and then fused onto a metallic surface. Some enamel is transparent and some opaque. Most enamel thimbles are made on a base of silver, copper or steel, with the sides covered in elaborate, decorative painting. The inside of enamel thimbles sometimes shows a whitish paint-like covering. This could be due to a repair, covering over internal cracking, but unless the outside appears too restored, one shouldn't be over concerned. It is inevitable, over 200 years, that a used thimble, designed as a fairly cheap souvenir, will show some cracking.

Enamel thimbles were never widely produced, and classic enamel thimble manufacture was limited principally to the eighteenth and nineteenth centuries, primarily in England, possibly gaining favor during these periods because enamel craftsmen saw it as a way to profit by copying the very successful porcelain designs of Meissen and their other European imitators. Certainly the style and patterns are very similar.

Foremost among the enamel thimble producers were factories at Bilston and South Staffordshire, in the English Midlands. Because there is no way of knowing if an item comes from Bilston, it is now considered more correct to refer to South Staffordshire enamels. Their work was copied, in turn, by some minor factories in Germany and France. Enamel thimble production still continues today in Norway and Germany, to a highly reduced degree; the thimbles are really manufactured only as sidelines by specialist enamelling factories.

There has often been discussion regarding the metal tops and rims of enamel thimbles. Were they always manufactured with them? Had they been lost over time? Or were some made without? Having handled and photographed so many now, I am sure that many were manufactured without. If you look at the painted decoration, it often extends right to the rim, the design would be spoilt with a metal addition. Regarding the top, it would require a different and more costly process to apply a metal top. It seems logical that you would either make a thimble with both metal top and rim, or one without either.

Enamelling is a decorative art which involves the covering of a metal surface with special types of glass in their molten form (more properly described as vitreous) and then firing the object to give a hard, glazed finish. The decoration thus achieved is particularly fragile, more so, even, than porcelain. It is very rare to find genuinely antique enamel thimbles in good condition. It is probably this delicacy which has prevented more thimbles from coming down to us from earlier periods.

All the enamel thimbles in the following section will be $1650+. The silver ones are $850+.

South Staffordshire English enamels, hand-painted. Left with metal top, right without.

South Staffordshire English enamel thimble without metal top or bottom bands.

Persian; right three: English.

Top and bottom bands in metal.

Left and above: Enamel thimbles.

Rare gold thimbles topped with steel.

18th century USA gold, but no identifying marks.

A little late 18th century gold thimble

Extremely rare silver gilt compendium with polychrome enamelled tailor on the finial. Each piece unscrews as in previous compendiums shown.

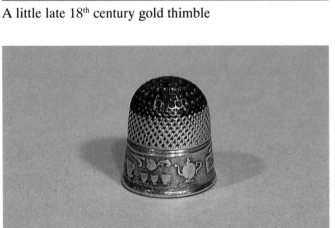

Very rare silver thimble with a border of teapot, tea cups, etc. and a steel top.

The famous "Freedom" tailors gold thimbles made in 1768, which fetched about $8500 a few years ago. *Photo courtesy of Sotheby's.*

Very rare border of greyhounds, a Renaissance influence. Probably Dutch, early 18th century.

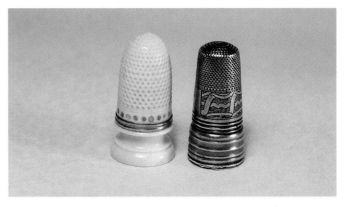

Both of these thimbles unscrew to reveal scent bottles. Left: ivory and gold; right: silver.

Silver with steel top, late 18th century.

The previous thimbles opened.

The same thimble for another view.

A silver thimble toy with scent bottle.

18th-19th Century Toys

(see text on page 38)

All the toys would fetch $1200 upwards. The compendiums in the case are $1350 upwards.

Toy with a scent bottle inside a thimble.

Left two: silver filigree thimbles which unscrew to reveal unusual blue glass scent bottle (center right); right: single filigree thimble.

Right: A compendium in its original case. Each part of the compendium unscrews. It was designed to contain needles, a powderer for your letters, a tiny thread holder inside the thimble, and, at the very base, initials which could be used to seal your letters.

A selection of filigree toys.

Enamel Copies

Antique enamel thimbles are so scarce today that it is a lucky collector indeed who has one. So perhaps of more interest to most collectors is the existence of a wide range of imitations.

The South Staffordshire factories were very successful, and as always in the world of thimbles, there were other companies keen to snatch some of this success for themselves. The moment one factory did very well with a product, other factories would pirate their designs and, in some cases, any identifying marks. This practice continued into the nineteenth and twentieth centuries. The imitators were not attempting to fake antiques, but rather to copy successful designs. The distinction between fakes and copies is not always very clear, however, and the subject of enamel thimbles is a controversial one in various ways.

Samson and Company, founded in Paris in 1845, was just one of the many companies that copied eighteenth century enamel designs, both as straightforward copies bearing their own Samson mark and as fakes, i.e. exact copies of the original eighteenth pieces, sometimes with their original marks. A comparison of an eighteenth century original and a later Samson copy will reveal that the brushwork on the original is freer and more fluent, that the enamel has more life and sheen, and that the colors on the thimble are not so powdery. As a general rule, the art of copying forces any artist into stiffness in reproducing detail accurately. Samson, among various companies in Europe also producing copies, issued their first replicas of eighteenth century enamel thimbles c. 1850. Copies of porcelain and enamel eighteenth century bibelots were also popular with the Victorian middle classes following the 1862 Special Exhibition of Works at the South Kensington Museum (now the Victoria and Albert Museum). Many replicas were made and indeed up until 1930, the Samson showrooms in Paris had rooms allotted to replicas of different periods.

Emile Samson was an acute business man and appreciated that his customers did not always want their copies marked as Samson pieces, as they wished to show them off as eighteenth century originals. Some pieces carried the crossed "S" for Samson, others did not (or the mark was removed by their later owners). Samson also reproduced and applied marks such as Meissen's crossed swords or Chelsea's red anchor if requested to do so by a purchaser.

Nineteenth and twentieth century copies of eighteenth century thimble holders lack the fine metal mounts or hinges and have a central metal "lug" (useful for identification on some thimble cases and egg-shaped étuis) to stop the lid opening too far. The mounts on the copies were often machined in a notched pattern on their outer edge. Samson and Company rarely used transfer prints on copies (unlike other European copiers), such was their pride in their freehand painting.

Samson copies continued to be made until they became too expensive for the customer. In 1975 a London antique dealer purchased the company's enamelling machinery. There is no documentary evidence to suggest that Samson definitely copied eighteenth century thimble designs. The only evidence is hearsay and the comparison of Samson pieces with earlier enamel objects. Shape alone is not conclusive proof of authentic or copied items, and testing of the metal under the enamel is both inaccurate and unhelpful, as there is insufficient data with which to compare the results.

In my opinion only an understanding of enamel plating, its application and the colors used, combined with a feeling for the period can give you enough confidence to date an object.

The Age of Enlgihtenment had seen the birth of the United States of America. Britain was prosperous and self-confident under George III, but about to be faced with revolutionary pressures from France and, eventually, Napoleonic wars. George IV was 48 when he became Prince Regent, a man of the arts. Indeed, the following regency period became a great age of elegance.

Chapter 6

Nineteenth Century Thimbles

Perhaps of all the centuries, the nineteenth was the age of optimistic progress. There was a generally held belief that a person was capable of anything, given health and the will to work hard, and that all progress was good. Samuel Smiles's "Self Help" booklet was the equivalent of the message of today's gurus and therapists "believe in yourself." This feel good factor of exuberance was echoed in all the designs of the time. The nineteenth century was without doubt the golden age of thimble design and manufacture. Queen Victoria and her able and popular consort Albert presided over a prosperous Great Britain and empire, succeeding George IV and William IV. Thimbles commemorating royal events, castles, day trips to holiday resorts and every romantic sentiment abounded. The ever improving methods of production made silver thimbles available to many.

In general, the first forty or so years of the century - roughly encompassing the French Empire and English Regency periods - were marked by a mood of cautious optimism, unlike the more carefree and comfortable decades that followed. This early watchful yet discerning temperament was reflected in the abundance of delightful, sometimes even frivolous - but rarely highly precious, as in the previous century - *objets de vertu,* including thimbles. High-quality but relatively affordable thimbles and sewing items, such as the mother-of-pearl Palais Royal type from Paris, were being produced on the one hand, while on the other, bone, Prisoner-of-War work, scrimshaw and Tunbridge ware were made as less expensive novelties. Strawwork, pen-work and scrolled paper examples were made, largely out of necessity and in the face of abject poverty throughout much of Europe. Many of the French prisoners taken during the Napoleonic wars were made to pay for their food in the prisons, earning the money by making items out of bone, wood and straw, hence the name "Prisoner-of-War" work.

By the middle of the century, however, times were getting better; the debilitating effects of the Napoleonic wars were diminishing and the overall European economy was improving. Concomitantly, the manufacture and popular use of thimbles made of precious metals increased, with silver, and two- and three-colored gold varieties especially favored, the latter often in sharkskin (also called shagreen, or *galachat*) cases. Brass and base-metal thimbles continued to be made in the 1800s, these generally mass-produced in huge quantities, and were of good quality considering their competitive price. The main producers were based in Germany in south Westphalia, and in and around Birmingham in England.

The development of the primarily nineteenth century phenomenon, the international trade fair, resulted in the display of thimbles from all over the globe, particularly European examples. These huge exhibitions were held regularly throughout the years in many locations, a significant proportion of them in France, but others in Great Britain, the United States, Australia and elsewhere. Local craftsmen would have been exposed to, and no doubt inspired by, the fine works on display at these fairs, thimbles among them. As a result, general standards of design and manufacture tended to rise.

Cut glass, very rare.

General Design and Construction

For about the first two decades of the century, the most common thimbles were domed like a beehive, their sides slightly wider than their tops, with fine indentations often reaching down the sides to meet decorative borders. One-part thimble construction was favored for silver and gold versions. From around 1830 thimbles grew slightly taller and lost their beehive shape. Fingerguards became very popular as well, and these were often offered in a set with a matching thimble. Some of the most refined sewing sets ever made date from this period, such as those in mother-of-pearl from the Palais Royal area of Paris.

Factory production increased markedly by the middle of the century, accelerating the decline of hand-made objects and making many talented craftsmen jobless. In Britain, especially, the rise of industry (including improved rail transportation) engendered the age of the mass-manufactured object, including thimbles, for general use. In general, from the middle of the century thimbles grew even taller and more decorative, retaining their slim shapes and rounded tops. The base-metal thimble took yet another blow, however, with the invention of the sewing machine. The industrial revolution, introducing affordable, mass-produced clothing for the first time, combined with the new facility for clothes to be machine-made at home, meant that eventually the demand for the humble working thimble (though not for its glamorous ornate counterpart) was to plummet dramatically.

Scottish Ware

Sewing tools such as needle holders, pin-cushions, shuttles and thimbles, as well as snuff boxes and various desk accessories, were made of three types of Scottish ware: Mauchline ware, Fern ware and Tartan ware.

The Mauchline ware industry was started by two brothers, William and Andrew Smith, of Mauchline, Ayrshire, Scotland. From the early 1820s they produced these delightful wooden wares, the earliest bearing painted and varnished scenes of famous local beauty spots. The direct application of paint on wood was replaced in the 1840s by scenes that were painted onto square or oval pieces of paper, glued to the wood and then varnished. Subsequent items were produced by direct transfer-printing and later (c. 1890) even monochrome prints were applied. Although most Mauchline ware, which was primarily intended for the tourist trade, was decorated with Scottish and English scenes, occasional export pieces with American, Continental or even exotic Indian or other colonial scenes were made.

Fern ware, dating from around the 1880s, was decorated with either ferns or ferns and shells. Early varieties tend to resemble fossil prints.

Arguably the most popular of these Scottish wares were pieces of Tartan ware, wherein tartan-decorated paper was carefully applied to wood surfaces and then varnished. Earlier pieces included hand painted landscapes set in tartan medallions. Later, such images were replaced by prints and photographs, sometimes of an important person or place within a tartan border.

Tunbridge Ware Thimbles

Tunbridge ware thimbles appeared in the early 1800s. Of simple turned wood such as yew or holly, these charming thimbles - which were originally tourist gifts made in Tunbridge Wells, Kent, a town whose well water was renowned for its curative powers - were often painted with delicate bands of red, green and yellow. Tunbridge ware usually took the form of boxes and games, with various sewing implements also produced. The later variety of Tunbridge ware, known as "stick ware," was also employed for thimbles, but such examples are extremely rare, as they were highly impractical to use (being made of small slivers of varicolored woods pressed together and coated with adhesive). On the whole, in fact, wood is not a good material for thimbles, since its softness makes it prone to split.

Early Tunbridge ware known as painted ware which came before stick ware. $500 plus.

A painted Tunbridge ware thimble with a flat top.

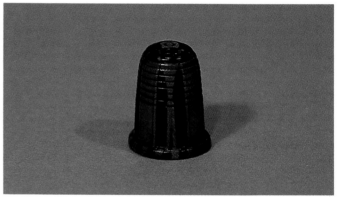

Rare Tunbridge stick ware example. It is known as the most expensive little bit of wood in the world, since it brought over $850.

A selection of early Tunbridge ware thimbles and thimble cases. At the back left is an example of stick ware.

Example of modern Tunbridge stick ware.

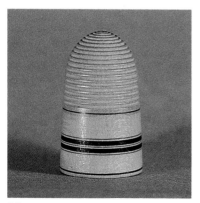

A painted Tunbridge ware thimble.

Gold Thimbles

Gold thimbles are not, in the main, hallmarked, so it is not very simple to ascertain the gold content, i.e., their carat. In general, however, Victorian thimbles were made in 15-carat gold, with 9-carat examples appearing in the late nineteenth century and made through to the beginning of the twentieth. The basic guideline to follow is that the heavier the gold, the higher the carat (though there are always exceptions).

In the nineteenth century, France and Switzerland generally used 18-carat gold (lower carats were not recognized as gold there), Great Britain used 9-, 15- and 18-carat gold, and the United States preferred 14- and occasionally 18-carat gold. German gold is accepted as low as 8 carats, but such pieces are more often of twentieth-century vintage.

Amazingly, there are 48 registered colors of gold (although you cannot discern the carat of gold by its color). The most common varieties are white gold (gold mixed with silver), rose gold (gold mixed with copper), green gold (gold mixed with various alloys) and pure gold, which is the 24-carat variety but it is somewhat rare due to its impractical soft state.

If a piece of gold does not have a hallmark (that is, carat mark), a professional jeweller can use the so-called acid test to ascertain exactly what the carat of the gold is or whether the article is merely gold-plated.

Instead of a hallmark, so-called convention marks often appear: 18-carat gold is marked "750," 14-carat is "585" and 9-carat gold is marked "375," and on imported goods, 22-carat gold is stamped "916," 18-carat "750," 14-carat "585" and 9-carat "375." Over the years, British gold standards have been lowered: up to 1798, 22-carat was the standard; from 1798 to 1854, 22- and 18-carat; from 1854 to 1931, 9-, 12- and 15-carat, and since 1931, 9-, 12- and 14-carat.

19th Century Plain Gold

All these thimbles will be $400 upwards.

Gold thimbles from Europe.

Gold Thimbles with Enamelling and Other Treatments

Persian enamel work c. 1830-1840.

Persian enamelling on 22 ct. gold, c. 1830-40 during the Qajar dynasty, the last Royal dynasty to rule Persia (Iran). A typical brilliantly colored flower design often found on jewelry of the same dynasty. $1350 upwards.

European enamelling of unknown provenance.

A Qajar betrothal thimble showing two portraits of the bride and, on the reverse, two of the groom. 22 ct. gold, c. 1830-1840. $2500+ depending on quality.

Enamelled borders. The top center is possibly American while the others are European. All upwards of $850.

Various gold thimbles. Note the early beehive shape of the thimble on the right.

A variety of gold thimbles.

A variety of gold thimbles. Left: an unusual cabochon top; center left: very rare possibly late 17th-early 18th century gold, botanical design.

Gold thimbles.

Gold thimbles. The center right thimble shows the famous Breton children dancing.

Gold thimbles. Center left: an unusual version of forget-me-nots; right: rare silver-gilt filigree, c. 1800. Upwards of $675 each.

A clutch of gold, stones, and enamelling. At the back center is an American grape motif.

60

Gold thimbles. The center right thimble has an interesting border.

Gold thimbles. The center right thimble has an enamelled name.

Gold thimbles with a variety of coral and pearl designs. Gold thimbles set with gems or enamelled, will fetch upwards of $600.

Gem-Set Thimbles

Many gold thimbles are set with real gemstones, which are generally colder to the touch than simulated stones made from porcelain, enamel, glass or early plastic. Some dealers test the authenticity of gemstones by biting them - they are supposed to be harder. I do not recommend this - it could cause dental problems. More crucial to the thimble collector than whether a stone is genuine or not, is whether it is in its original setting. A replacement stone, even if it is intrinsically valuable, takes away from the authenticity of a piece, thus lowering its quality and its value to the collector.

Victorian thimbles often contained so-called "jewels," which were, in fact, drops of porcelain or colored enamel (usually reminiscent of coral or turquoise) or bits of glass (resembling amethysts, garnets and the like). Interestingly enough, real turquoise is porous and prone to discoloration, so the pretty, evenly colored blue stones imitating the gemstone are often thought of as the real thing, and the actual, often discolored stone is falsely assumed to be the fake. Semi-precious agate and cornelian were often used instead of glass in stone top thimbles, particularly since they were then nearly as cheap as glass.

19th Century Gold with Gems

All these thimbles will be upwards of $675.

English set with garnets, cabochon style (unfaceted).

*Right:*Fleur de lys set with turquoise.

Amethyst lozenge-shaped.

Intricate interlacing border set with turquoise.

Unusual combination of pearl and onyx.

Diamonds and rubies.

Intricate applied border inlaid with garnets.

Unusual hand-punched dimples and carnelian top. Possible Scandinavian.

Unusual pearl rim.

Alternate pearls and faded corals.

Gold and turquoise, with tiny garnet centers in Forget-me-not pattern. Note the earlier beehive shape.

Alternate slanting bands of pearl and turquoise.

Blue enamelling, possibly French. Note the flat top.

Turquoise set band.

Two thimbles spelling out the word "Regard" in gems: R for ruby, E for emerald, G for garnet, A for amethyst, D for diamond.

Enamel buckle design very popular in mid-19th century, showing a Saracen influence.

Left: Forget-me-nots in turquoise; right: turquoise.

Late 18th-early 19th century thimbles. Note the pepper pot shape with high domes.

A variety of mid-Victorian gem set thimbles.

Châtelaines, Étuis and Boxed Sets

Châtelaines, étuis, nécessaires, sewing boxes and various other containers or accessories can greatly enhance a thimble collection. A châtelaine, which hung from a clasp or hook suspended from the waist, comprised several chains supporting separate items such as a thimble in a case, scissors or a notebook and pen. An étui, on the other hand, is a single container in which a variety of items is held; it can be portable, for carrying in a pocket, or simply kept on a table, like a smaller sewing box. Étui cases are often elaborately decorated and can be of gold or pinchbeck mounted with, for example, tortoiseshell and malachite or mother-of-pearl.

Nécessaire is a general term covering any small container, including a sewing box. In the 1880s the leather-boxed sewing set, or nécessaire, was extremely popular throughout Europe; an English example from the time comprises a leather case with a silver-gilt sewing set inlaid with corals.

Châtelaines have the longest ancestry of these accessories; their history can be traced back to early settlements. Over the years they fell in and out of fashion. A man's version, the "Macaroni," was particularly popular with eighteenth century dandies, and was commonly worn in pairs, on either side, attached to the belt. These were used to carry a watch, keys, and seals. A wide variety of châtelaines were in great demand throughout the nineteenth century, from the Romantic period of the 1810s (when medieval and Renaissance revival designs of gold, pinchbeck, cut steel and silver were made), to the time of the Great Exhibition of 1851 (where these "amusing little trifles" were noted with wry amusement by a writer in the *Illustrated London News*), and to the 1890s, when cut-steel and silver versions proliferated.

Boxed sewing sets were made not only in Europe, but also in the East, as evidenced by an unusual 18-carat gold Indian set of the nineteenth century, almost certainly made by the Pertabgarh workshops in Rasputana, northern India. Beautiful enamelled plaques fashioned by local craftsmen sometimes adorn the boxes which enclose a thimble, Indian or otherwise, and scissors.

Sewing Boxes and Sets.

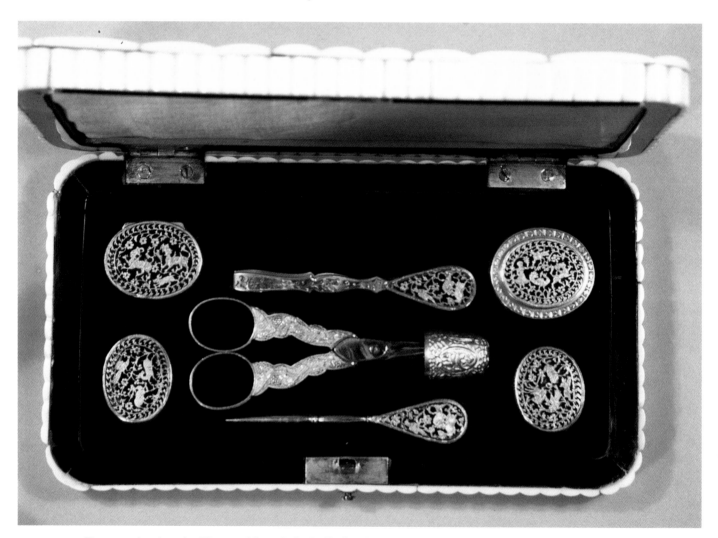

Rare sewing box in 18 ct. gold made in India for the British Raj, c. 1840. It comes from the Petrabgarh region famous for pierced gold jewelry backed by red or green mica. $5000.

Early 19th century French set of Damascened tools.

Enamel on copper, European, probably c. 1840.

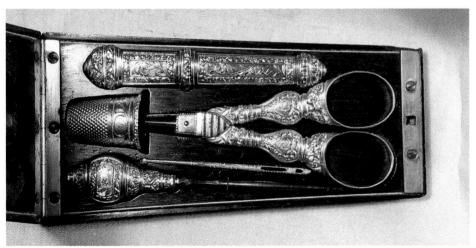

A wooden case with a French, early 19th century set of 18ct gold tools. $1,120.

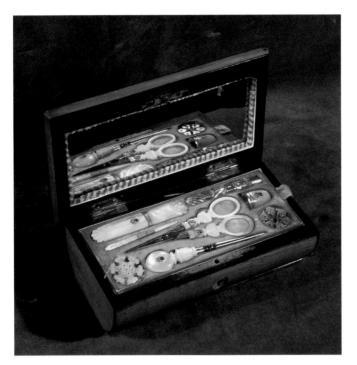

Box lid of sewing set showing Arab influence in interlacing designs.

Thimble Holders

Thimble holders, or cases, are delightful objects and desirable to many collectors with or without their contents. It is due to them that so many vintage thimbles are in such excellent condition today, the owner(s) having kept the thimble in its original case, which itself can be quite attractive and decorative. In the eighteenth century, the finest thimbles were often contained in shark-skin (also called shagreen, or *galachat*), tortoiseshell, ivory or gold cases, with the humbler varieties encased in vegetable ivory, Tartan ware and other assorted materials. The Victorian period is especially rich in unusual thimble holders, with examples shaped like boots and shoes, eggs, suitcases, even ships with the thimble attached to a mast. Beside the common wooden varieties, thimble holders can be made of pressed glass, leather, porcelain, gilded metal, even mother-of-pearl, the latter two lined with silk or plush.

Thimble Cases, Sewing Compendiums, Boxed Sets and Chatelaines

Wooden box set with mirror, c. 1800, typical Palais Royal, with mother of pearl tools. $3,204.

Sewing compendium, early 18th century. $1200+.

19th century silver chatelaine set. $1040.

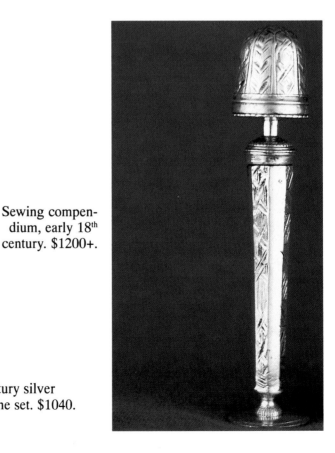

Ivory thimble case banded in gold, unscrews to reveal gold thimble, c 1830. $700.

Left: tortoiseshell thimble holder, c. 1840; center: ormulu thimble holder, c. 1790; right: combined needle and thimble holder in tortoiseshell, c. 1840. $350 each.

South Staffordshire enamel needlecase and thimble holder with painted pastoral scenes, c. 1780. $1000.

Ivory and gold compendium, c. 1830, with silver and steel topped contemporary thimble. $425 for the compendium.

Mother-of-pearl egg, opening to reveal gilded metal tools., c. 1850, probably French. $500.

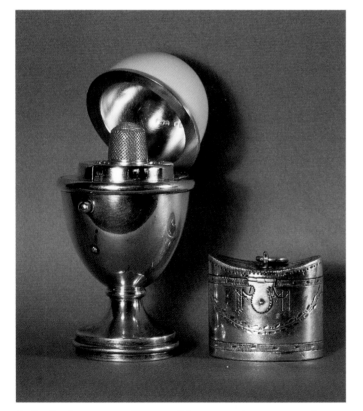

Left: An important silver and ivory sewing compendium showing thimble and pin holder. Hallmarked London, 1875, it has Russian initials on base, and provenance suggesting that it belonged to Princess Alexandra. Right: late 18th century novelty hat box thimble holder. $500.

Three silver thimble holders. Left: USA; right two:
English. $325+ each.

Gold thimble set with sapphires and diamonds with
matching mother-of-pearl octagonal holder, c. 1850.
$675+ set.

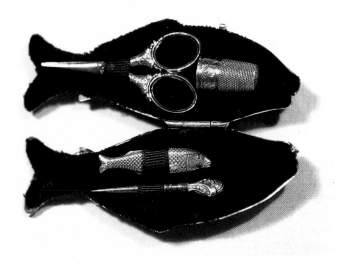

Opened, the fish sewing set measures approximately 12
cm. $640.

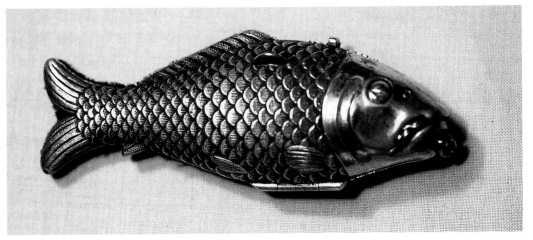

Novelty little fish sewing
set in silverplate, c. 1840.

Thimble holder with equestrian motif, c. 1850.

Enamel on silver holders, c. 1920s. $250 each.

Typical glass shoe thimble holders, $100.

Hat box in leather novelty holder, $100.

Novelty compendium, thimbleful enamelled on silver. These little measures were used to drink from. Their name "thimbleful" is derived from a woman's typical reply to "will you have a drink?" "Thank you, just a thimbleful." $425.

Examples of thimbleful spirit measures.

Possibly French novelty thimble holder. $135+.

Palais Royal Thimbles

One of the most desirable thimbles the experienced collector wants to own is a Palais Royal. Exquisitely delicate, it is made from mother-of-pearl and named after the palace in Paris originally built in 1629 for Cardinal Richelieu (as the Palais Cardinal) and occupied in the late eighteenth century by the powerful Duc d'Orléans. Members of the Duke's entourage required especially luxurious articles for their toilette, travel and other needs, so talented craftsmen in the vicinity of the palace were employed to provide these pieces. Sewing boxes fitted with lovely mother-of-pearl accessories were among the articles made by these workshops, with the thimble usually assuming a dome shape, encircled with two gilt bands at the base. Each sewing tool had a tiny oval plaque containing a blue and green enamel pansy, flower, or sometimes a butterfly, set in gold.

Today it is easier to find individual Palais Royal accessories rather than complete boxes, but remember to look for any cracks in the mother-of-pearl. These thimbles have often lost their oval plaques or had them replaced with a plain gold version. In fact, there were mother-of-pearl thimbles made with plain gold plaques, but these were usually in the shape of a shield. Mother-of-pearl is a very seductive material, because of its irridescent sheen. If you can imagine a drawing room, lit by candles, the soft reflecting colors of a mother-of-pearl thimble, deftly plied, must have lured many a gentleman to the sewer's side.

The legendary mother-of-pearl Palais Royal thimble with central cartouche in gold and enamel, showing a pansy which stood for pensez-a-moi or "think of me." $875 plus.

Ivory Thimbles

Ivory thimbles have long been popular, particularly in France, more perhaps for their delicacy of design than their efficacy in sewing. The earlier ivory thimbles were beehive-shaped, and sometimes finished off with a gilded band. Later varieties often came from China or India, where they were sometimes part of a fitted lacquer or ivory sewing box made for export to Europe. Some of the Oriental thimbles comprise two parts and can be unscrewed, the upper being threaded onto the lower body. Plain ivory thimbles were used to sew pure silk, as they did not snag.

The growing scarcity of ivory in the nineteenth century encouraged the use of corozo or coquille nuts, both also known as vegetable ivory, for thimbles and other accessories. The former is usually slightly darker than real ivory and has a distinctive, waxy finish, whereas the latter is darker still and was used more for thimble cases. Ironically, vegetable ivory thimbles may cost more than ivory examples as they are difficult to find today.

"Dieppe" work is finely carved ivory and derives its name from the French port on the Normandy coast where, as early as the fourteenth century, large quantities of ivory were imported from West Africa. From the seventeenth century, Dieppe carvers were renowned throughout Europe for their ivory articles, and such souvenirs were especially popular with Dutch and English tourists. Although sewing items did not comprise the bulk of these carvers' output, there are many examples of carved ivory pin-cushions, waxers, shuttles and fans. Small pieces are usually unsigned, although some of their makers imitated medieval craftsmen by carving their "mark," such as an eye or hand, onto their creations. Very fine carved ivory thimbles are rare, and much sought after.

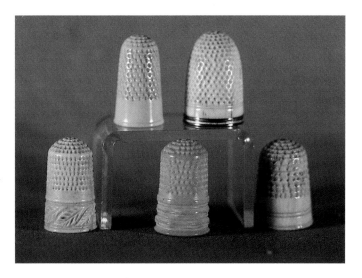

The center thimble is vegetable ivory, the others ivory.

Ivory with very finely carved border, possibly French. $675 plus.

Left: vegetable ivory; center: glass (very rare); right: most unusual border of ducks, probably Dieppe work from France.

Ivory thimbles. Left: probably English; center two: probably Asian; right: French with gilded bands in the same style as the mother-of-pearl shown earlier.

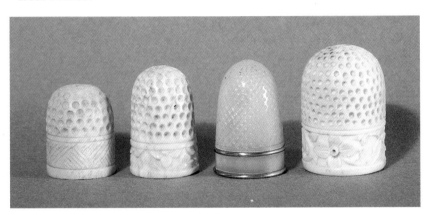

A very fine example of Dieppe ivory work.

Left: Chinese ivory thimble for European market; center left: Indian ivory thimble for the European market; center right: mother-of-pearl French Palais Royal with gilt bands and without pansy; Chinese ivory.

Left: Chinese ivory; center: undecorated ivory made for sewing silk; right: French or English ivory.

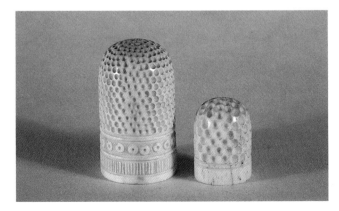

Both ivory thimbles made in Asia for the European market.

Left: part of a 17th century thimble holder probably bone, base missing; right: early 19th century ivory set with steel.

Left: could be an ivory and silver Dutch "convent thimble," the only possession a girl was able to take with her on entry; right three: English vegetable ivory.

Tortoiseshell Thimbles

Among the most popular Victorian thimbles was the famous "Piercy's Patent," which was made of tortoiseshell combined with gold, silver or a combination of both. Such thimbles usually have a metal top, with circular punches and a tortoiseshell body. The classic Piercy has a crooked shield flanked by a lion and a unicorn (British heraldic beasts), often with the words "Piercy's Patent" inscribed underneath. Many variations of this design occur. The patent was registered c. 1816.

A most attractive variation is a pinchbeck cert-o-let outer sleeve with a tortoiseshell lining. Tortoiseshell thimbles are also found in Europe, especially in the Netherlands. A good tortoiseshell and gold example can command up to $595.00.

Left: Shagreen (fish skin); center: finely carved ivory; right: vegetable ivory.

A tortoiseshell banded with gold saying "Piercy's Patent" with a rare steel top. It is the reverse of the left thimble in the photo at right. $3375 plus.

Left: Tortoiseshell and gold, probably English; center left: iron and gold, a favorite combination, made by the French; center right: Palais Royal; right:ivory in the Palais Royal style

Typical example of the famous Piercy's Patent. $3375 plus.

British Thimbles
Victorian Silver Souvenirs
of Places and Events

In the mid-nineteenth century, Victorian England was at peace, relatively prosperous and at the dawning of the age of the manufactured object. Although the rise of the sewing machine rang the death knell of the common, utilitarian thimble, the production of fancy silver and porcelain models flourished.

Hand in hand with rapid industrial growth in Victorian Britain was the rise of public transportation. Railroad lines began to criss-cross and trail up and down the country, taking eager tourists to such places as Windsor Castle, Brighton Pavilion and the Great Exhibition at the Crystal Palace in London's Hyde Park in 1851. The increase in travel and tourism sparked a souvenir trade, and with it the production of the souvenir thimble. Such thimbles might feature portraits of royal residences or pictures of castles, the designs of which were manufactured as ready-made die stamps or as decorated skirts, which were wrapped around the sides before the top was soldered on.

Left: Dublin Exhibition; center left: place name of Cheltenham; center right: place name of Dover; right: Sir Walter Scott's house.

All these thimbles will be $850 to $1350, depending on condition and rarity.

Left: Lichfield Cathedral; center left: unknown souvenir showing boat on a river; center right: Windsor Castle; right: another view of Windsor Castle.

Left: Newstead Abbey; center left: unknown; center right: the Tay Bridge; right: Brighton Pavilion.

Four views of the Great Exhibition in 1851.

A third version of Brighton Pavilion. This was built by the Prince Regent before Queen Victoria's accession.

Left: Brighton Pavilion; right: Brighton Chain Pier.

A fourth rare version of Brighton Pavilion.

Unusual upside-down version of Brighton Pavilion.

A rare version of Brighton's Chain Pier.

Brighton Chain Pier.

Lichfield Cathedral.

A different view of Windsor Castle with the word "Windsor."

Rare version of Windsor Castle on a fingerguard.

Another castle, possibly Windsor, one of the Queen's residences.

A further version of Windsor Castle on just a border.

A different version of Newstead Abbey.

Extremely rare Balmoral, the Queen's highland home.

Dover Castle.

English Silversmiths

Thimbles were made by various silversmiths of the nineteenth century and in great number. Although each thimble may not carry a hallmark (and accompanying initials of the maker), a great many of them do. The following silversmiths and com-

panies were the principal makers of thimbles in Victorian Britain:

Joseph Taylor, 1773-1801, Birmingham. While he did not produce large numbers of thimbles during the time he was in business (late eighteenth to early nineteenth century), Taylor made fingerguards and also patented a brass non-slip thimble. The initials J.T. are sometimes found under the handles of small basket pin-cushions. The initial I is often used on marks in lieu of J.

Charles May, London. Firm existed from 1805 to 1929; thimbles usually quite plain.

George Unite, 1832-1901, Birmingham. Unite and J. Hillard registered the mark "G. & H." on 8th August 1832. Unite's own mark, "GU," was used 1832-61, and from 1873-90 the same mark was used by William Oliver Unite, Edward Willoughby Unite and George Richard Unite, who traded as George Unite & Sons. From 1890-1927 Harry Lyde traded as George Unite & Sons, and the company became George Unite Sons & Lyde in 1928, when the punch "GUS & L" was adopted (until 1931, when it was cancelled).

James Fenton, 1852-1923, Birmingham. Firm traded mainly from *c.* 1852 to 1900. First registered mark in November 1852. Further punches registered between 1860 and 1882. Last entry was for January 1885, and Fenton died in 1886. In March 1885 Fenton's son-in-law Samuel John Boosey became proprietor of the firm, trading as James Fenton (continuing same mark). In May 1890 Alan Howard Elkington and Walter Bolding replaced Boosey as proprietors and continued using the Fenton mark. Last mark recorded in December 1923.

Henry Griffiths & Sons Ltd., Leamington Spa. Traded mainly from 1886 to 1955. Founder Henry Griffiths worked until 1916, when his sons took over the business and formed a public company. Son Fred, who joined the firm in 1880, is supposed to have given the name "Dreema," after his daughter, to the popular thimble (which rivalled Charles Horner's Dorcas model). Fred Griffiths died in 1951; firm continued making thimbles until 1955.

Charles Horner, Yorkshire. Firm traded in the late

19th and early 20th centuries. Hallmarked mainly in Chester. Silver production ceased in 1925, but Dorcas thimbles continued. *See page 99.*

Walker & Hall. Manufactured a thimble similar to Dorcas and Dreema, called "Dura," which is fairly rare today. Yet another manufacturer (unknown today) made the rare sister "Doris" model.

Joseph Addis. Existed from 1828-1885.

James Collins. 1828-70

James Webb. 1843-90

Francis Clarke, Birmingham. 1830s.

James Swann. 1837-1922, mark registered in 1887. The addition of "& Son" was made in 1922 when his son took over and continues today. Mainly assayed in Birmingham.

Olney, Amsden & Son. A late nineteenth-century firm, whose mark was "O.A. & S." Makers of the blackberry pattern, among others.

English Silver Hallmarks and other Stamps

Most English silver thimbles before the 1890s are not hallmarked as they fall below the required weight. If your English silver thimble is hallmarked, it should always be stamped with a lion, which denotes that the silver is of sterling quality, i.e., .925 or 92.5% pure. The next stamped device indicates the town where the article was assayed, the most common being London's leopard's head, Birmingham's anchor, Chester's three corn sheaves and Sheffield's crown. This device is followed by the date letter, which is enclosed within a shield or cartouche and indicates the year of manufacture. These three marks may be followed by the maker's initials. Various highly detailed handbooks can be purchased explaining these terms and identifying the dates represented by the date letter.

Some thimbles also contain registered numbers, which originated from the Patents Design and Trade Marks Act of 1883. The numbers are consecutive from 1883 and reached 600,000 by c. 1910, allowing for approximately 20,000 designs

a year. Thus a thimble with registered patent no. 222445 should date from c. 1893. Remember, however, that the date of the registered design is not always the same as the date of manufacture of that particular thimble.

The Britannia silver quality mark was introduced by William III in 1696 to prevent the coin of the realm from being melted down to make plate. The quality of plate was changed to the higher grade of .958, and the figure of Britannia in profile indicates this higher standard of silver; it is used on coronation commemoratives even today.

There is another mark relating to patents applied to articles, though it is rarely found on thimbles except for some made for the Great Exhibition of 1851. The mark is a diamond-shaped lozenge and was used in England from 1842 to 1883; it indicates that the design had been lodged with the London Patent Office. In 1884 the diamond mark was superseded by a row of numbers, for example 012345. So, if a piece bears the diamond, it is 1883 or earlier; if there is a registered number, it dates from 1884 onward.

General Victorian Silver Thimbles from the 19th Century

Bright cut decoration in the manner of silversmith Samuel Pemberton, c. 1820. $170+.

Similar Pemberton-like design on rare fingerguard. $220+.

A group of early 19th century fingerguards. These guards were worn in order to exert pressure from the side of the thimble rather than the top.

Another group of guards. Sometimes guards were used on one hand in conjunction with the thimble on the other.

Silver with steel top for heavier sewing, c. 1820. $135+.

A gadget known as The Trueform made in silverplate.

Very rare rebus thimble, meaning "stick to me."

Silver thimbles, c. 1830. The center thimble is a rare early souvenir of Brighton. $425+.

Rare bicycle thimble made by James Fenton.

In the past these thimbles were thought to be Indian, but recent evidence shows that they are 19th century English. $250+ each.

Left: blackberry design by James Fenton, B'ham 1900; center: a different blackberry, also by James Fenton B'ham 1896; right: another James Fenton thimble, 1914.

19th century English silver. $250+.

19th century English silver. $250+.

Pierced cable style border. $100+.

Rare bell-shaped thimble. $135+.

Unpierced cable style border. $110+.

Another bell-shaped thimble. $135+.

Pierced cable border. $125+.

An example of the cable thimble. A similar one is on view at the Science Museum in London.

Applied flower border of unusual sparkly design. $135+.

Unusual English thimble, unmarked. $100+.

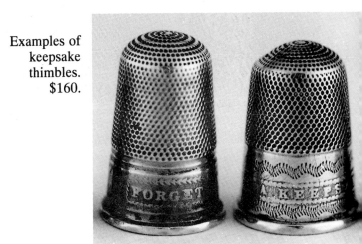

Examples of keepsake thimbles. $160.

Rare, richly decorated border. $200+.

Above, above right and right: More examples of keepsake thimbles. $160.

Another rare thimble with a beautiful border. $200+.

A group of typically English 19th century designs. At the left and right of the bottom row is the famous blackberry design. The two in the center of bottom now are German.

Silver border of thistle with a stone top made by James Swann. $135.

Various stone tops. $100 each.

The Harp with a Connemara marble top, by J.Swann B'ham 1899.

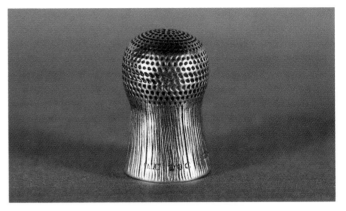

Variations of cable borders with stone tops. This is a very unusual combination. $135+ each.

Silver with stone tops. $100+.

This thimble has a rare engraved border of fish. $135+.

One of the most legendary silver thimbles ever made. Hallmarked 1893, pat. no. 222443. The design is of a thistle. $1500+.

Very unusual border, unmarked. $150+.

Enamel on silver, unmarked. $250+ each.

Enamel on silver.

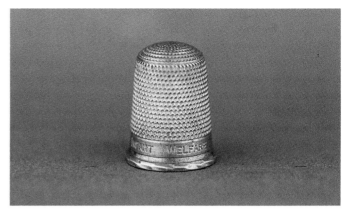

Rare motto for "Infant Welfare."

Group of English thimbles. Note the brass child's thimble with steel top, top left.

Group of English thimbles. Note the child's pewter thimble, bottom right.

Group of the Dreema thimbles made by Henry Griffiths. They were introduced as a rival to the Dorcas thimble made by Charles Horner.

The Dorcas thimble in its original box. The Dorcas is constructed of a silver outer layer, a steel inner core, and a silver inner lining. These thimbles were said to be indestructible.

The very rare Little Dorcas.

Left: By Henry Fosket, London, 1881; center: no mark c. 1870; right: very unusual clasped hands.

A group of Dorcas thimbles all by Charles Horner.

Very interesting porcelain painted plate with a very unusual border of thimbles. Origin unknown.

Commemorative Thimbles

Silver royal commemoratives became very popular in the nineteenth century. Two of the first were made for the 1831 coronation of William IV and his wife (one bore the words "Long Live King William IV", the other "Long Live Queen Adelaide"). Numerous commemorative thimbles were issued to celebrate births, marriages and other events connected to Queen Victoria and her family, including her ascension and coronation in 1837 and her marriage to Prince Albert in 1840.

Plated Victorian Commemoratives

Most plate or brass Victorian Commemoratives have an estimated value of $300+.

Rare Victoria's Jubilee thimble, silverplate.

Three thimbles celebrating Queen Victoria, possibly for her Jubilee, silver plate.

Left: "The Queen's Record the Best of All," a thimble brought out during the reign of Queen Victoria; center: rare good luck thimble; right: Victoria, again in honor of the Queen. Sivlerplate.

Rare early commemorative, "Long Live Queen Adelaide" married to William the Fourth, c.1830.

The Queen's Record, enlarged. Silverplate.

Victorian Commemoratives, mostly silver

All Royal commemoratives from about $850 upwards, depending on condition.

Royal Events

The reverse sides of the thimbles below left.

Thimbles commemorating events in Victoria's life and reign. Left: wedding; center left: coronation in 1838; center right: Silver Jubilee; right: Diamond Jubilee. Queen Victoria was born in London on May 24, 1819.

A picture of Victoria and Albert, c. 1850.

Three silver commemoratives. Left: Victoria's accession in 1837; center: her wedding to Albert in 1840; right: profiles of Victoria and Albert.

Three thimbles celebrating Victoria's wedding to Albert in February, 1840.

The birth of the Prince of Wales in 1841.

Left: Victoria's accession in 1837; right: her marriage to Albert

The birth of the Princess Royal in 1840.

Left: another marriage thimble, with a portrait of Albert; right: Albert and Victoria.

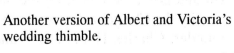

Another rare version celebrating the Birth of Prince of Wales.

Another version of Albert and Victoria's wedding thimble.

Left: a rare view of Osborne House, one of the Queen's residences; center: Queen Victoria's Jubilee; right: The Great Exhibition of 1851.

carried on by J.D. and C.H. Horner. The original Dorcas was made until 1905, at which time new, improved Dorcas thimbles were introduced (under the name "Improved"). The pat. and registered design numbers were later dropped; subsequent thimbles were stamped with the name "Dorcas," mark "CH" and size number. By 1925 silver production ceased and only the Dorcas continued in production.

The "Improved Dorcas" was also made in 9-carat gold with the same steel lining as the silver model. "Gold Dorcas," "Little Dorcas," and "Junior Dorcas" specimens are all extremely rare.

Close up of the Queen's Jubilee of 1897 thimble, with its central portrait of the Queen.

Rare brass commemorative, "Victoria" in raised letters.

Charles Horner and the Dorcas

Charles Horner, of Hebden Bridge, Yorkshire, and later Halifax, is well-known to thimble enthusiasts for his steel-lined thimbles, later called Dorcas, which he patented in 1884 (pat no. 8954). Between 1887 and 1890 many patents were issued.

The original Dorcas thimbles did not carry the name Dorcas, rather just the registered design number (rd. no.) or pat. (abbreviation for patent). The earlier Dorcas had a domed cap, whereas later ones often had flat tops. The Little Dorcas came later; whether the Junior Dorcas was a version of the Little Dorcas, or a later development, is not known.

Charles Horner also made thimbles in solid silver and gold, these bearing the initials "CH" and usually the Chester assay mark. In 1896 the firm's founder, Charles Horner, died and business was

Charles Horner silver thimbles from 1890 to 1910.

Charles Horner silver
thimbles from 1890 to 1910.

Charles Horner silver
thimbles from 1890 to 1910.

Charles Horner silver thimbles from 1890 to 1910.

Selection of Dorcas thimbles. In good condition they should cost from $25 upwards.

Left to right: the Dorcas, the Dreema, the Little Dorcas, the Dorcas Junior and the Dorcoid.

A rare Charles Horner thimble with the raised letters of the place name Llandudno.

Very rare C. Horner pierced Persian lace pattern.

All Charles Horner products showing various designs such as the very rare Dragon and Cupid thimbles. All these thimbles were auctioned in the late 1980s in mint condition, having been found in his old workshops. The rare designs, including the Dragon and possibly the Cupid, will all now fetch over $325. An ordinary design, in good condition, of any 19th century thimble will cost $45 upwards.

British Base Metal Thimbles

Brass Working Thimbles

The rise in popularity of the sewing machine meant the beginning of the end of the thimble. Many thimble manufacturers closed down during the nineteenth century, especially those providing "working thimbles" of base metal to clothing manufacturers. Still, numerous companies survived, or even started up to produce thimbles for industry, among them Edwin Lowe Ltd., a London firm trading from 1852 to the mid-twentieth century. Lowe exported thimbles to the United States and also produced them for the Royal Army Clothing Department. The firm no longer makes thimbles today, although it still exists as a maker of other metal items.

Charles Iles established his firm in 1840 and won an award for his thimbles displayed in London at the 1851 Great Exhibition. He also received prizes at the Kensington Exhibition (1862) and Brussels Exposition (1877). The firm experienced even greater success in the next century, doubling its production by the 1920s and producing aluminum (or alurine), plastic, nickel and chrome-plated thimbles through the 1960s.

Both thimbles and needles by Abel Morrall & Co. were exhibited at the international exposition in London in 1862. The thimbles are marked either "Abel Morrall" or "O.A.S." Thimble production ceased in the late nineteenth century, but the firm continued to make needles as part of the Aero group.

Everyday thimbles in brass. The second from the left has the border inscription "remember me" and the middle one is inscribed "forget-me-not."

Brass thimbles. Left: French advertising; right three: English, the second from the right inscribed "Her Majesty" (Queen Victoria) on the border.

Selection of late 19th century English everyday thimbles. Border design is an imitation of silver.

Brass thimbles. The left thimble has a threader device, and the next is a boudoir thimble.

Brass peep thimble. These peeps or Stanhopes contained miniature pictures of places in the apex.

Child's pewter thimble. This is an unusual thimble material owing to its softness.

English Porcelain Thimbles

English porcelain thimbles experienced unprecedented success in the nineteenth century, and today they are among the most desirable types of thimbles sought by collectors. The richest period for such thimbles is from the late nineteenth to the early twentieth century, although every collector should also be familiar with the earlier designs, styles and marks (as you never know when you might happen upon a rare treasure). The Worcester factory provided the largest number of thimbles, but it is known that Wedgwood produced at least a small number of thimbles at their Etruria works, though only for about a decade from the late 1790s.

The prolific Royal Worcester porcelain factory was established in the eighteenth century, but its thimble production was greatest in the late nineteenth and early twentieth centuries. Early in the 1800s the Japanese Imari influence (1800-10), exotic bird designs (1810-15) and flowers and landscapes (1815-70) were rife, but seldom have these been found on thimbles (although the Smithsonian Institute in Washington, D.C., owns Worcester thimbles decorated with landscapes). From 1870 to 1930 floral designs continued in use, and there were numerous avian motifs as well. Thimbles with white, blush ivory or peach backgrounds often feature bird or floral patterns; jewelled patterns featuring droplets of coral and turquoise were also popular. Many of these continued to be made through to the present century, although today thimble production has ceased. Never wash an old Worcester thimble, because the paint is not protected with a glaze.

Early Worcester thimbles are not often marked, mainly because of space restrictions, so the collector should become familiar with the detailed brushwork, elaborate gilding and highly translucent porcelain that were so characteristic of the factory. Although nineteenth-century painters were not allowed to sign thimbles, it is known that Read and Hopewell were among Worcester's thimble decorators in the Victorian period. After 1900, signatures began to appear.

The late nineteenth-century Worcester thimbles that are marked contain a puce mark indicating that they were made after 1891. The puce mark gave way to a black mark after 1938. The factory used a dating code from 1862 through the 1960s, but it was seldom applied to thimbles. Rather, a special small mark was used for the thimbles, though it was not altered every year.

The only other English factories producing Victorian porcelain thimbles that can be identified were in Derby. The Bloor Derby factory closed down in 1848, but its former employees started up the firm Stevenson & Hancock soon after; the factory operated until 1935. The mark "S & H" is found inside some but not all of these Derby thimbles. Another Derby factory which made thimbles was the Royal Crown Derby Porcelain Company, which in fact took over Stevenson & Hancock in 1935.

The center right thimble is probably not Worcester. It could be Coleport.

Left: the squat-shaped earlier type of Worcester; center left and right have the peach background known as blush Worcester.

19ᵗʰ Century Royal Worcester Thimbles

The following thimbles are probably all Royal Worcester, dating from the 1870s to the 1940s. In general early Worcesters go from ???250 upwards (depending on condition), and later ones are ???190 and upwards. Hand-painted Worcesters from the 1960s to the present (black mark inside) are ???20.

The second thimble from the left shows typical fine white paste which resembles opaline when held to the light. The second thimble from the right has an unusual flower design in the earlier squat shape. If you have the chance, buy the translucent paste examples, especially with the richer gilding. They will be upwards of $500 each.

Note the robin in the center. The reverse holly will be seen in a later photo.

In the back row, the left three are possibly Coleport. Note the fine flower design on the center right thimble in the back.

The right thimble has the very rare Worcester subject of a butterfly.

Various birds on blossoms.

Left two: blush Worcester; center right: unusual flower design; right: squat shape.

Left: blush Worcester; center left: squat shape; center right: very well-painted insects and flowers with rich gilding; right: unknown, possibly Coleport.

Left to right: blush; fine white background; flowers on blush, unusual; squat.

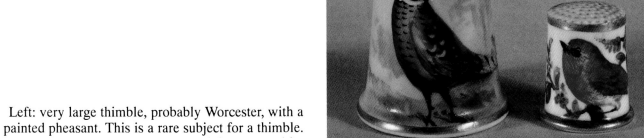

Left: very large thimble, probably Worcester, with a painted pheasant. This is a rare subject for a thimble. Right: squat robin.

Various birds. Note the more intricate gilding on the center left thimble.

Left three: blush Worcesters; right: white ground with slightly later shape.

Left: blush; right three: white background. Note the different position of bird from usual profile on the center left thimble.

A variety of birds and one possible Coleport (center right).

These all have Worcester's purple mark inside. All the earlier Worcester's have no mark inside. Left: signed Mosley; center left: Powell; center right: Mosley; right: "jewelled" drops of porcelain to imitate turquoise. Purple marked Worcester's were the first to bear artist's signatures. George Mosley was one of the famous group of artists known as the "terrible seven." Ted Townsend was another, who also painted thimbles. They all joined Worcester together in the 1920s and used to play cricket down the length of the painting shop. Their rivals were the Saucy Six, all girls, amongst whom, the Rea sister, Daisy and Nell, painted thimbles.

All purple marked inside. The center left thimble is marked Powell. William Powell, born 1878 & at the factory from 1900-1950, has become one of the sought after painters, not just because of his fine painting, but his appeal as a character. William was born with a badly deformed spine, but his lively spirit charmed the visitors to Worcester's factory. He mainly painted birds, with delicacy and detail. Today they will fetch over $325 each. Originally he asked 6p for a painting. When he got too old to complete all his orders, Ted Townsend did them.

All purple or puce marked inside. Note this period is much thicker in the paste and is not translucent. The shape is bigger and the painting not as detailed. The center right thimble is signed by Powell.

Various birds. $420+ each.

Unusual subject of wren.

Robin.

Note rich lattice gilding on the transparent white background.

Examples of rich gilding on opaline type background.

Early signed W. Powell. Unusual subject of swallow.

Various unmarked birds.

Worcester unmarked, unusual flowers. $500+.

Worcester unmarked, unusual flowers. $500+.

Made by Locke & Co.showing the arms of the town. $500+.

Squat thimble, probably Worcester, with unusual flowers. $500+.

These have an estimated value of $500 and upwards.

Derby. $850+

Interior showing crossed swords under a crown and SH for Stevenson and Hancock.

Rare Derby with Imari pattern, inside SH mark. $850+.

Possibly French, typical blue band. $500+.

Unusual half gold background and flower border. $500+.

Very fine white background showing violets richly gilded, possibly early Worcester. $500+.

Early 19th century English thimble, no mark, with typical Regency stripes decoration. $500+

English unknown maker, unusual gold background with morning glory and other flower. $500+.

Unusual full-blown roses on blush, probably Worcester. $500+.

Possibly French, unusual design of dots. $500+.

Left: possibly Coleport, note the typical straight sides; right: probably Worcester. $500+.

Probably all early 19th century English porcelain of unusual designs. $500+ each.

Blush background, probably Worcester with unusual raised white stamens to the flowers. $500+

Left: early English porcelain; right: painted ivory, c. 1830. $500+ each. *Courtesy of British Museum.*

The following will bring upwards of $500 with some going as high as $1350.

Left to right: French; Worcester; English; Derby with S & H mark inside. $500+ each.

Unusual early English porcelain designs. $500+ each.

Left: rare highly-decorated Imari pattern by Derby; center two: probably Worcester; right: possibly Coleport. $500+ each.

Porcelain thimbles, the one on the right is the rare wild strawberry design, possibly Worcester. $500+ each.

Jewelled Worcester with white background. $500+.

Left: Meissen; right two: Worcester. $500+ each.

Two elaborately decorated early English porcelain. $500+ each.

Left: English; center left: immensely richly gilded Worcester; center right: Imari Derby; right: reverse of robin showing holly. $500+.

Left: unusual pepper pot shape, early English; center: French; right: early English. $500+ each.

Three examples of Worcester jewelling in unusual arrangements. $500+ each.

Jewelled Worcester thimble with unusual diagonal bands. $500+.

Worcester jewelling with especially rare use of green on the center thimble. $500+ each.

Other Worcester jeweled thimbles with a similar green jeweled piece at the left. $500+ each.

Worcester Jewels on a blush ground. $500+.

French Thimbles

In the nineteenth century, thimble production in France encompassed gold, silver and the lovely Palais Royal mother-of-pearl types. Thimbles were exhibited at French trade fairs as early as 1819 (in the Palais du Louvre), and in 1834 examples by Mathieu Danloy earned a bronze medal at the Paris Exposition. A. Feau was an established manufacturer specializing in gold and silver thimbles; not only did he display his wares in Paris (in 1878), but he also showed them in Sydney (1879), Melbourne (1880), and Amsterdam (1883). Another well-known French thimble designer was F.P. Laserre, whose creations were sometimes signed "LAS RRE," the "RRE" below the "LAS."

One of the most renowned silver thimble designers in France was Frederick Charles Victor de Vernon, a metallurgist and sculptor who created thimbles for both P. Lenain & Co., and Maison Duval in Paris. A celebrated Vernon design, in the popular *fin-de-siècle* Art Nouveau style, was known as "The Sewing Girls." It was illustrated in *Les Modes* in April 1909 and may have been designed to celebrate the marriage of the Dutch Queen

Wilhelmina in 1900 (it bears the boar's head mark, for Paris). A thimble of the same design was later produced as part of a leather-boxed sewing set, along with scissors and needlecase, by Maison Duval (one can be seen in the British Museum); it is marked "J.D." (for Julian Duval), whose tenure with the firm lasted from 1893 to 1925). Vernon also designed thimbles featuring characters from the famous La Fontaine *Fables* and Perrault's fairy stories, originally dating from the 1890s and reissued *c.* 1910-20 (and again in the United States in the 1970s). Vernon deliberately chose seventeenth century shapes - complete with waffles - for these sets, since both the fables and fairy tales were written in that century.

Unlike English thimbles, whose rims are generally plain, French thimbles of the nineteenth century, except for those by Vernon or Laserre, feature decorated rims. Otherwise, French thimbles are usually similar in construction.

The French hallmarking system on needlework tools is called *petite garantie.* A cock appears on gold and silver before 1838 and a rabbit's head on

Paris silver from 1819-1838. Parisian silver after 1838 carries a boar's head, provincial silver a crab, and imported goods (of silver or gold) a swan. Gold thimbles after 1838 should bear an eagle's head (or a horse's head, if provincial up to 1919). An owl identifies objects otherwise unmarked from 1893. French thimbles are becoming more appreciated now, owing to their beauty of design.

"Paris," $350.

Left two: exhibition souvenirs, $250 each; right: border of mistletoe $135.

Handsome art nouveau designs, $175 each.

Souvenir thimble, $135.

Left possibly souvenir from Lourdes, $250 each.

Souvenir thimble "N 'Oublions Jamais" after World War I, , $135.

Thimble with applied rococo border, $175.

114

Three floral borders, over $175 each.

Sewing woman, $425+.

Two thimbles showing a sewing girls theme, $425+.

Shell design, $135.

Art nouveau designs, $250+ each.

Rare border of ginkgo flowers, $250.

The famous French fairy tale designs by Vernon. $475+ each.

Applied flower border, $135.

Left and right, various sewing girls, center, English. $450.

Cherry border, $200.

Gold with raised applied border, $350.

Flower border, probably by Laserre who shows a crisp, strong design. $200.

Left: French; center and right: unmarked, possibly German.

Flower border, $200.

Gold, $270.

A copy of the famous fable or fairy tale thimbles brought out in the United States in a limited edition, 1980s.

Gold, fairy tale or fable. $675.

Raised flowers, $170.

Left: one of the famous fable series, Joan of Arc; center left: another of the fable series, two love birds; center right: a later version of the love birds; right: a raised border of cones.

Early 20th Century French Thimbles

This is the box for the French war thimble. I am not sure if there were not two types, one to commemorate the Battle of the Somme in 1916, and another one for the end of the war.

A close view of the thimble on the previous page. Note signature Las-rre under the soldier.

1914-18 commemorative, also by Laserre. $500

Another 1914-1918 thimble.

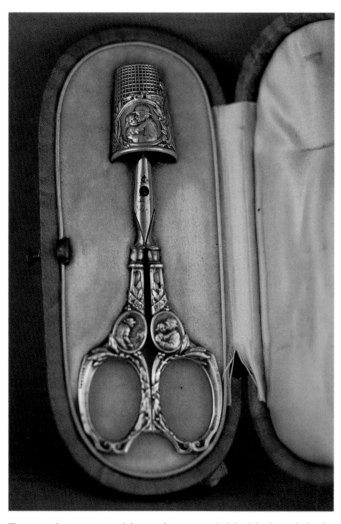

Extremely rare matching scissors and thimble in original box, 1914-1918. $1200.

A closer view of the 1914-18 thimble at left, known as *Le Dé de la guerre*.

German Thimbles

The most prominent nineteenth-century thimble manufacturer in Germany was Johann Ferdinand Gabler, a tailor's son born in 1778. Gabler started up the business in 1825 and it reached its peak in 1914, when Gebrüder Gabler employed some 150 workers. The firm produced gold, silver, brass, nickel and aluminum thimbles over the years. Early Gabler thimbles were sometimes marked with a "G" in a rosette, whereas some later models incorporated an eight-pointed star-shaped pattern at the top; some, however, were not marked. Competition was fierce among German thimble makers, so designs and marks were often copied, among them Gabler's star-shaped top.

Gabler manufactured hundreds of different types of thimbles, with such elements as enamelling, shields, initials, stone tops or stone skirts added to the basic shape. Some late nineteenth-century examples were decorated with curvilinear Art Nouveau (or Jugendstil, as it was known in Germany) motifs. Gabler thimbles were available in .925 or lower-grade silver, the cheaper type giving Gabler or other German firms an edge in the export trade, but, in general, lowering the overall quality of output. Some of Gabler's top quality thimbles entered the Russian Royal Collection, whereas the majority of them were intended for the general market.

The Gabler thimbles that were exported to Russia included models which often carried the Russian hallmark of "84" or "88" on their rim, but they should not be confused with indigenous Russian examples. Likewise, exports to Scandinavia were marked with assorted hallmarks of those countries, thus making for, at times, confusing similarities between thimbles coming out of Germany, Russia and Scandinavia during these periods.

Among the other German thimble makers were Frederich Eber of Pforzheim, a firm that existed until 1980; Soergel & Stollmeyer of Schwabisch-Gmund; Helmut Grief of Winterbach and Wilhelm Lotthammer of Pforzheim. The latter firm operated from 1850 to 1969, and published its catalog under the name of Lotthammer & Stutzel. Windmills and country scenes of blue and white enamel often appear on Lotthammer's silver thimbles, mistakenly suggesting to many collectors a Dutch origin. However, the star-petal top indicates German manufacture, and the windmill-decorated versions were probably made for export.

Lutz & Weiss, Eber & Pranol and the Johann Moritz Rump Company all produced thimbles in Germany in the nineteenth century but only Rump does so today. In 1845, Rump produced 12,000 gross metal thimbles! The firm has recently published a booklet illustrating its early thimble designs.

Few porcelain thimbles are known to have been made in nineteenth century Germany.

German and Dutch

Beautiful German silver thimble with enamel pansies by Gabler.

Close-up of 84 hallmark.

Various silver and stone-set German thimbles.

Three German enamel on silver thimbles.

18th-19th century German or Dutch thimble.

Silver thimbles with stone tops.

Left: "Happy Family" design. On the right silver with steel top, c. 1790, English.

As a very general guide, most German thimbles made by Gabler have an eight petalled or star top. Those made by Lotthammer have a six petalled top. This is a photo of German thimbles from 1890 to c.1910.

Possibly Dutch, c. 1810.

Various German thimbles, probably by Gabler. The one on the extreme left shows a Russian mark of 84, possibly for export.

Andersen, decorated with reindeer, polar bears and fjord scenes.

Some of Andersen's older thimbles have moonstone tops, with enamelling covering guilloche-style, engine-turned silver, whereas examples from the twentieth century have silver-gilt waffle-shaped tops. The Andersen firm still produces enamelled thimbles today. The turn of the century thimbles, especially those featuring a Scandinavian scene, are now important collectors' items.

Austrian Thimbles

The most distinctive nineteenth century thimbles made in Austria were attractive silver examples with raised decoration. Many of these were unmarked, but those that were marked included a number on the front indicating the "Loth," that is, the standard unit of silver purity used in Germany, Austria and much of central Europe. The numbers "12" and "13" represented .725 and .825, respectively. This system of marking was discontinued c. 1860.

Scandinavian town souvenir thimble.

Silver 800 hallmark from Austria.

Two possible town souvenirs with stone tops.

Scandinavian Thimbles

Of the Scandinavian countries, which generally imported thimbles from abroad, Norway evolved its own distinctive gold and silver thimbles, some with stone tops and finely engraved straight sides, others enamelled, others undecorated. Enamelled thimbles were a Norwegian specialty, with early silver and silver-gilt examples sporting enamelled border designs and later examples, such as those by the Oslo silversmith David

Silver with stone tops, unmarked, probably German.

Silver with stone tops, possibly Norwegian.

Unmarked gold thimble with steel top.

Silver and enamel David Andersen thimbles. The center left thimble is 19th century; the others are 20th century.

Gold with steel top, c. 1790-1800.

Gold thimbles with stone tops

Gold with onyx top.

Selection of enamel on silver, most probably by David Andersen.

Gold with gold wire work decoration and moonstone top.

David Andersen, enamel on silver.

Enamel on silver with the rare design of a swan.

Reverse of swan thimble.

Enamel on silver thimbles, also by David Andersen.

More David Andersen enamel on silver thimbles.

Russian Thimbles

Russia is such a vast country that each province has a different history. In the south of Siberia, each Tuval woman had a pouch of fur or leather to hold her thimble and needles. Sewing tools are important in the nomad's life, and are often found buried in their graves.

In the Volga region, the local women used to decorate their clothes and headdresses with thimbles. They also hung them from a shoulder holster, made in the same fashion as a man's ammunition holster. This might explain why the silver cartridge case tops look like thimbles: they were perhaps influenced and made by the same manufacturers. The Kirghiz women wore their thimbles on the back of their headdresses in the same way as the Turkumans. In many Russian communities in the past, it was the custom to bury a woman with her thimble and needlework tools. In the town of Lithua all the graves containing various tools were burnt during a raging fire, the only items that

did not burn were the thimbles. I am indebted to Helen Predein for this information.

Russian thimbles generally fall into one of three distinctive styles: niello, enamel and a form of applied cut card work. Souvenir thimbles from the Caucasus often bore names in Cyrillic script and were decorated in the niello style, wherein a black design is etched onto a silver background. Such thimbles are not as costly as the famous Russian enamel thimbles, on which polychrome enamel is laid between little wire reserves on a ground of silver-gilt or gold. The finest enamel thimbles demonstrate subtle variations of shading, such as the light pink on the inside of a flower blossom darkening at the edge of the petals.

Not all Russian silver thimbles are hallmarked but if they are, the hallmark is found on the rim with either "84" or "88". Until 1925 the Slothnik was the Russian unit of purity applied to silver, with "96" representing pure silver. From 1896 to 1907 a woman's head facing left was sometimes used on Russian silver, and from 1908 to 1917 a woman's head facing right, but such marks are rare on thimbles. After 1927 the "84" changed to "88" or ".875".

The more marks on a piece of Russian silver, the more important that piece, so four marks - for instance, "84", the factory name, the town where it was made and the maker's initials - denote a significant item of silver. The size of thimbles, however, precluded the use of many marks, and it is the number alone that is found most frequently. Beware, however, of recent copies or fakes bearing the "84" on their rim; the workmanship on such thimbles is usually quite poor. The number 56 denotes the mark for St. Petersburg, found on gold thimbles c.1880.

Silver and enamel thimble from just after the revolution. $225

Russian

Niello work Cyrillic script, souvenir from the Caucasus area.

Silver and enamel thimble with 84 pre-revolution mark. $675.

Left two: enamel on silver with 84 pre-revolution mark; right: souvenir.

All pre-revolution Russian thimbles. $675 plus.

More pre-revolution Russian thimbles. $675 plus.

Silver with raised flower design probably from the Caucasus area. Note similarity to cartridge tops. $250.

Cartridge holder from Russia with silver top, which you can see is much longer than the thimble shown previously. The thimble on the left is for scale.

Left: a pre-revolution thimble. $675+; center: unmarked, probably not Russian; right: post-revolution thimble. $350.

Production of thimbles in the United States reached its zenith at the end of the nineteenth century. In general, thimbles of this period retained the shorter shape of the eighteenth century, the only changes being apparent in their indentations, which became larger and assumed a uniform roundness.

Most American thimbles from this time exhibit both a firm grasp of design and quality workmanship, although they were less variable in design than their European counterparts. Silver examples from 1860 onwards usually bear the word "STERLING" or "STERLING SILVER".

Porcelain thimbles were not widely produced in North America in the nineteenth century, but collectors should be on the lookout for the factory names Ott and Brewer and also the Ceramic Art Company, both from New Jersey and both of which manufactured porcelain thimbles at the end of the century. Notable American thimble manufacturers included the following firms:

Right: unusual shape, note 84 mark on rim. $590; left: this is either a fake or copy from the 20th century.

Simons Brothers & Company, Philadelphia. George Washington Simons founded his company in 1839 in Philadelphia although it was not named Simon Bros. For over 40 years, George, his brother and four sons ran their business from the Old Jones Hotel - which they refurbished and renamed the Artisan Building - in Chestnut Street from 1864. The company won a medal for its excellent thimbles at the 1876 Centennial Exposition in Philadelphia.

Simons Bros. thimbles are marked with a Gothic "S" inside an upturned bell or shield, a mark they had used from the 1880s onwards but did not register until 1907. It appears on both their gold and silver thimbles and is still current today. A smaller trademark generally indicates an earlier thimble. Simons Bros. have reissued their thimbles for collectors, and the reissues, some of them dating from the 1890s and made from the original dies, are almost as sought after as the first issues of the same models.

Three Niello examples probably on Afghan borders. $350 each.

Ketcham & McDougall Company, New York. Existed from 1832 (when it was founded as Prime & Roshore) to 1932 as jewellers. Hugh McDougall joined the Ketcham firm, located in New York, in 1857, although it was not until 1875 that the partnership between him and Edward Ketcham was formed (prompting the change of name to Ketcham & McDougall). The company produced a variety of items including thimbles which were marked with the MKD trademark from its introduction in August 1892. Some of the earlier thimbles carry the patent mark "Sep 20, 81". Ketcham & McDougall made thimbles from many metals including steel, silver and gold and was the first American company to market aluminum thimbles. They stopped making thimbles in 1932.

P.W. Lambert & Company, New York. They produced oxidized silver and "Egyptian Gold" thimbles, châtelaines, ladies belts and other goods from the middle of the nineteenth century onwards.

Untermeyer-Robbins. Existed from 1890 to 1930, after which time it was bought by Stern. Mark "UR".

Stern Brothers & Company, New York. Operated from 1868-1933. The Stern family emigrated from Munsingen in Germany, arriving in Philadelphia in 1863. Nathan Stern worked for Henry Muhr and Sons before starting his own business at 63 Nassau Street, New York. The Stern Bros. catalog in 1890 advertised a complete list of thimbles: from 1890-1908 these bore the company trademark of an anchor with a rope twisted around it. Collectors will recognize later thimbles by their trademarks: an "S" with a "B" in its upper curve and a "C" in its lower curve was used on thimbles from 1908-12. A "G" enclosing an "S" and a "C" marks thimbles produced between 1913 and 1933, the "G" representing August Goldsmith who had become a partner. The stock market crash of 1929 hit Stern Bros. badly and the business shut down in 1933.

Waite Thresher Company Limited, Providence, Rhode Island. Daniel Waite established himself as a silversmith in Providence in 1860 and was joined by a new partner, Henry Thresher, in 1884. Their early thimbles (*c.*1886-*c.*1906) are marked with a star inside the top; later thimbles (*c.*1907-*c.*1927) are marked with a thimble inside a star.

Waite Thresher stopped making thimbles in 1927 and sold their designs and machinery to Simons Bros.

H. Muhr and Sons, Philadelphia. Operated from 1873-1894. Mark: a crown.

Nineteenth-century American thimbles are perhaps underpriced in comparison with English thimbles and this is a good time therefore for collectors to look for interesting items to add to their collection. Good American thimbles can sometimes be bought for less in Europe than in the United States of America.

19ᵗʰ Century USA Antique Silver

An unmarked thimble of unusual shape and design.

Rare unmarked thimble with the motto "A Merry Christmas."

Rare unmarked Mizpah engraved "The Lord watch Between Thee and Me When We are Absent One from the Other."

Unusual brass thimble with silver lining.

Left: Silver with applied gold bands, fused onto the silver, by Simons brothers; center: the same type by Stern Bros.; right: another by KMD. These applied gold borders or bands are an entirely American invention. $75 each.

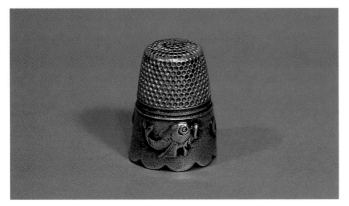

Very early aluminum in imitation silver with a border of fish.

Various silver thimbles with two gold ones on the left. The general shape of the American thimble is always stubbier than in Europe, and has not altered over time.

Washington by Ketcham and McDougall Company, c. 1895, a souvenir.

Silver with applied gold borders by KMD. The one on the right is a typical pattern of flutes between panels. The gold fluted bands cost twice as much as the silver. $75 each.

Reverse of Washington thimble.

Simons Brothers thimbles. Center left is the famous cupid patent, dated Nov.21, 1905. $325. Center right is the raised vines pattern known as grape, pat. July 9, 1907. $150.

Left: Simons Brothers; center left: unmarked; center right and right: unmarked, but showing Florida, pat no. .08 81.

Various makers in 1890s. $45-55 each

Waite Thresher Company Limited thimbles. The center embroidery thimble has very rich scroll designs. The scroll was used more by Waite Thresher than others.

Simons thimbles.

Simons thimbles.

KMD thimbles.

Thimbles by Goldsmith and Stern, a later amalgamation with Goldsmith. From the early 1900s. Typical designs of rural landscapes were often used.

Thimbles by Simons, one of the most prolific manufacturers, with many different designs.

Stern Bros., a later thimble manufacturer.

Unmarked thimble with an unusual border.

Gold by KMD. $100-120.

Ketcham and McDougall thimble with rare enamel border of holly berries. $200.

Tailor's ring.

USA: Antique Gold

Gold with steel top c. 1820. $200.

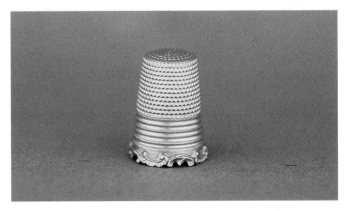

No mark, very pretty rim. $240.

Simons thimbles showing various engravings. The scenes in the center left and right thimbles are typical of Simons.

A gold thimble set with tiny pearls.

Various unmarked gold thimbles.

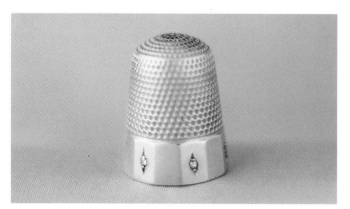

Single gold thimble set with tiny diamonds.

Unmarked thimble with well engraved border.

Two thimbles by KMD with raised wild roses.

Rare USA thimble of an unknown subject.

134

Reverse of previous thimble.

Unmarked thimble with unusual border.

Another unusual, unmarked piece.

Golden cherubs. $400.

Left and right: Mesopotamia; center: Marsh Arab. Note the date of 1918 on the right thimble. $135+.

Marsh Arab thimbles, $100+.

Mesopotamia and Marsh Arab thimbles.

Mesopotamia and Marsh Arab thimbles. $100+ each.

A Marsh Arab thimble. $100+.

A Marsh Arab thimble. $100+

Thimbles from the Near and Far East, Greece and Turkey

Occasionally nineteenth-century thimbles from Armenia, India, China and other oriental countries become available in the West. Examples from Afghanistan, for instance, have recently come out of that country. Such thimbles are usually worn by women as jewelry, either attached to a finger ring or worn under their head veils. They are part of a woman's dowry.

Armenian thimbles of silver or gold with black niello-type decoration are known, and black and silver niello thimbles have come from the Mesopotamian region (in present-day Iran and Iraq).

India produced handsome repoussé silver and gold thimbles in the 1800s, many versions with scalloped or wavy edges. Such decorated thimbles were imported by the British Army & Navy Stores, and were also intended for the domestic market, primarily for the British Raj in India. Some British firms even copied elaborate Indian designs, and there are cases of Indian-made thimbles receiving English hallmarks.

Various designs made in India for the British Raj mid-19th century.

Mid-19th silver thimble made for the British Raj.

Turkish thimbles, $50+ each.

Mid-19th century Indian thimbles.

137

Note the very attractive curved border on these Indian thimbles. $150.

An encrusted all-over floral design.

A different style of wavy border with raised repoussé flowers.

Chinese, Nomad and Greek

Antique shops in Hong Kong have yielded silver or enamelled silver sewing rings; some of these have been authenticated as nineteenth-century antiques by specialists in Chinese enamelling and silver design. It is possible that the very beautiful rings that we thought were for sewing are scarf rings. We cannot be sure as yet. Certainly the Chinese used sewing rings, often the expandable variety, which they still use today. The Mandarin nail-guards that one sees are a reminder of the days when an aristocrat had to be seen never to lift a finger!

The end of the nineteenth century really saw the end of great thimble production. The sewing machine caused the decline of hand sewing, but so many women must have been glad of its labor saving power. Beautiful thimbles will always be made, but now they are the exception rather than the rule.

Silver and enamel Mandarin nail-guards from China.

Persian silver thimble decorated with roses.

Nomads from Afghanistan and surrounding areas used rings with thimbles attached as dowry pieces. They sometimes suspended them from their head-dresses. $350+ each.

Left: a modern Chinese sewing ring; right: old Chinese sewing ring. Both are expandable.

More Afghanistani pieces.

Enamel and silver Chinese sewing rings, $250+ each.

More Afghanistani pieces.

Enamel and silver Chinese sewing rings, $250+ each.

More Afghanistani pieces.

Expandable Chinese sewing ring.

Center: thimble attached to a ring. $290. On the right is a gold thimble set with malachite. $300+.

Left two: gold set with malachite; right two: silver thimbles.

Left two: gold set with malachite; right two: silver set with malachite.

Greek silver thimble decorated with enamel.

Greek silver decorated with enamel.

Rare 22 ct. gold amulet with thimbles and rings attached, all set with malachite.

South American gold. South American thimbles very often have a flat top. $430+.

Silver thimbles from Afghanistan.

141

Chapter 7

Twentieth Century Thimbles

The twentieth century will be viewed as the age of skepticism. The Victorian era had seemed full of certainty, with the belief that hard work and increasing prosperity were going to give everybody a better life and all progress would be beneficial. After Queen Victoria's death in 1901, Britain was one of the foremost nations in the world. Edward VII and Queen Alexandra came to the throne of a powerful Empire in industrial and technological ascendancy. A commemorative thimble was made for the coronation in 1902, but these thimbles are very scarce, only a few plate ones remain. The golden age for commemoratives had past. Many royal events during the reign of Queen Victoria had been celebrated with fine commemorative thimbles, but by the twentieth century both the desire for thimbles and the veneration for royalty had decreased.

At the dawn of the twentieth century, the restraints imposed by Queen Victoria were thrown off, and for the brief period known as the Edwardian Era, England enjoyed a time of frivolity and fun, epitomized in the spirited dancing figure of the Gaiety Girl. The fashion in Edwardian home furnishings was the revival of the neo-classical style popular in the eighteenth century. Motifs such as garlands, swags of flowers, and cupids were used to decorate everything from furniture to thimbles. Pretty silver boxed sewing sets, decorated with similar motifs, were brought over from the Continent, mainly France. King Edward loved the joy of life that he found in the café-filled boulevards of Paris, so the French influence in the decorative arts was strong, especially with the aristocracy. The French sets were more feminine and ornate than their English counterparts. There is still nothing to surpass the thimble designs of Laserre and Vernon; the figure modelling and tiny exquisite scenes really are works of art.

Edward's reign was short, and because his children were born whilst his mother was still Queen, there were no commemoratives made to record their births. The eldest son, George would become king on his father's demise, and as children so often do, George was determined to be a very different monarch from his father. George epitomized the British Naval officer, reliable and steadfast.

Blunt King George V and his unbending wife Mary came to the throne in 1910, which they jointly occupied throughout the First World War until the King's death in 1936. There were many silver and brass thimbles made to commemorate their coronation. The most attractive and easily recognizable one is in silver, chased with a view of Buckingham Palace, the coronation coach and Westminster Abbey with an applied gold crown and the legend G.M.1911. Then came the horror of World War I, which meant that all production was geared towards the war effort. In Britain there was no equivalent of the 1914-18 war thimble designed by the great Laserre, which in rare cases is found together with matching scissors in a small leather box. The nearest equivalent was one enamelled with red, white, and blue concentric rings, bearing the legend "A Stitch for The Red White and Blue," and later "Infant Welfare and Peace 1919" in silver, hallmarked J.F. in Birmingham 1918. The next royal commemorative thimble made was to celebrate the silver jubilee of King George and Queen Mary in 1935. It is interesting to note that some bear the dates 1910-1935, and some 1910-1936.

After King George's reign of 26 years, his son, Edward, abdicated in 1936 before his coronation. In one of the great modern romances, Edward gave up his throne in order to marry an American divorcee, Mrs. Wallis Simpson. The only thimbles that I have seen relating to Edward's coronation have been in the form of a hussif-a thimble, cotton holder and needle case combined-made in a cheap gilded metal. Instead of the social, debonair Edward, his shy and stuttering brother King George VI and his consort Queen Elizabeth were crowned in 1937. The coronation silver thimble was very simple in design, owing to the hasty change of sovereign, and as few were made it is also rare. It bears simple initials either side of a small crown. Some nickel-plated thimbles were also made with "Coronation G.E. May 1937, King George VI Queen Elizabeth," which are even rarer. There were now only three years to go before the unthinkable happened: World War I had been the war to end all wars, and now we were preparing for World War II. As far as Britain, France and America are concerned, there do not seem to have been any thimbles made to commemorate events concerning World War II. The time of the mass use of thimbles in everyone's household was past.

King George VI and Queen Elizabeth were the parents of our present Queen Elizabeth II, so the next royal commemorative was made in 1953 for the coronation of the Queen on the death of her father. There were two versions made in silver, one is fairly plain, the other follows the basic design of her grandfather's in 1911. There is no record of a commemorative being made in 1947 to celebrate the Queen's marriage to Prince Philip. During her reign, a thimble was issued for the investiture of Prince Charles as Prince of Wales at Caernarvon Castle in 1969, and a handsome silver thimble was made to celebrate the wedding of Princess Anne to Mark Phillips in Westminster Abbey in 1973, although recently this so-called nuptial thimble has been called into question. The same design, but without the 1973 hallmark has been re-used since. Prince Charles married Lady Diana in St. Paul's Cathedral in 1981, and several thimbles were made to mark the occasion. The British royal commemoratives have been listed on their own, separate from general thimble development, in order to make their sequence clear. So now we will return to the early twentieth century.

After the turn of the century, Art Deco was all the rage, and the Jazz Age had arrived with its clear influence on all the decorative arts. The 1920s planted the seeds of modern living, and mass-production played an ever-increasing role in everyday life. The German equivalent of the Art Deco movement, the Jugendstil, was running its own course of modernization in Europe. The designs were generally heavier than their French equivalents, and rarely used on thimbles. The mass-production of aluminum (or, to give it its older name, aileron) thimbles was developed for advertising purposes, with the thimbles employed as a giveaway token (Iles and Gomme have recently decided to reissue certain aluminum advertising thimbles through a mail-order catalog in Great Britain). The twentieth century saw the growing invention of the gadget thimble, usually made in cheap metal; there were cotton cutters, wire threaders attached at the side of the thimble, and magnet tops to pick up your pins and needles. The nickel finger-shaped thimble was patented in England by H. Bourne in 1904, and led to the "Trueform" thimble which was made in silver, brass, nickel and later in plastic. Other gadget thimbles included the expanding plastic wrap-around finger-guard, the telescopic folding metal and the ventilated thimble, with ivorine lining.

Celluloid has also been employed in the manufacture of thimbles since the last years of the nineteenth century; some are of solid celluloid while others have celluloid linings. The non-slip celluloid thimble was patented c.1936. Collectors often have trouble telling plastic from ivory: plastic often has a glassier sheen. If you own the thimble, you can prick it with a hot needle, and compare the smell it gives off with another plastic object. Some of the prettiest plastic thimbles were painted with cupids and one in good condition is well worth having. In the United States plastic thimbles began to be used for advertising purposes.

The 1960s and 1970s saw the mass-production of inexpensive china thimbles with transfer prints to meet the demands of the booming travel and tourist industries. Although these souvenirs are interesting, they should not be mistaken for antique hand-painted thimbles, nor looked on as an investment. The exceptions to this rule are commemoratives, which are always worth collecting as usually few were made. If you can get a hand-painted one all the better, but buy a printed one rather than not have one to remember the event.

Many companies have discontinued the manufacture of porcelain thimbles (among them Spode, Wedgwood and Royal Worcester). Less reputable entrepreneurs have sought to exploit the collector's love of the subject and the market has been infested with special issues and collector's sets of thimbles that have little value, intrinsic or otherwise. There are special issues still being made by some of the major companies. Sometimes made for the overseas market, these are worth having. Wedgwood made a very attractive set of the Kings and Queens of Britain for America. Also worth having are the more unusual Wedgwood basalt colors, such as yellow, or terra-cotta.

Advertisements can be seductive but the point to look for is whether the design is hand-painted or printed: if it is printed then the thimble may not be well finished and so less likely to appreciate in value. If an advertisement does not clearly state whether the thimble is hand-painted or printed, call the manufacturer to clarify the matter. Most contemporary china thimbles are rarely likely to prove a good buy if you are collecting for profit, as well as pleasure. Be warned: a huge collection of mass-produced modern thimbles, which had been advertised for sale in limited editions as "antiques of the future" and assembled by their owner at a cost of over £2400 ($4000), recently sold for only £200 ($340). Again there are always exceptions, one of these being the relatively modern set of china thimbles brought out by the Derby factory. The set was never completed so no-one is sure how many there should be!

Some modern thimbles are well worth purchasing, however. Good craftsmen and artists deserve to be supported. Names such as Graham Payne, Peter Platt, Ken Russell, Nigel Creed, Jasper's of Yorkshire, and some of the best Russian painted wood thimbles will be sought

after in the future. Shirley Frost made some of the finest modern silver thimbles, her commemoratives being especially highly prized. A wonderful silversmith, winning many a design prize, sadly she had to retire early owing to arthritis. Kay Kendall Thetford modelled superb miniature animals on silver thimbles, and has now gone on to sculpt in bronze. James Swann and two women silversmiths, Jane Chantler and Ailsa McKenzie, are continuing in a dying industry of hand-crafted thimbles. Peter Swingler must rank as one of the great miniature painters of our time, and his Monarchs of Britain series will be one of the great collections of the next century. Christopher Bowen is another silversmith to look out for. He has designed a lovely golden wedding thimble, celebrating the 50 year marriage of Queen Elizabeth to Prince Philip. Kuo-Chi Lin, a famous fashion designer, has designed a stunning picture of Hong Kong's skyline on a thimble. It commemorates Britain's secession of Hong Kong to China in 1997. As a general rule, silver commemoratives have the advantage of a hallmark which identifies when they were made; fine hand-crafted silver and porcelain thimbles as beautiful as any antiques are still being made and can be collected My collecting tips for the future are as follows. First, read as much as you can on the subject, then join your nearest thimble collecting society. Shared knowledge is so helpful and much more fun. Collect as many old thimbles as you can, alongside good modern commemoratives and individual designs of high quality.

Now, as we are amazingly near the close of the

Left: four thimbles with printed designs by Caverswall; right: "Sweetheart." $16.

twentieth century, collectors are getting together more easily, owing to greater ease of communication, and telling the stories behind some of their thimbles. It is incredible to hear how far some thimbles had travelled, linking friends worldwide.

That is one of the joys of collecting, because you end up with not only a collection of thimbles, but also a collection of collectors who can teach you much about their own cultural history encapsulated in the thimble.

Needle holder, thimble holder and thimble in hand-painted, ormolu mounted, Limoges.

Transfer-printed Caverswall (English china).

Russian, hand-painted porcelain.

Royal Worcester transfer-printed animals.

Left to right: Chinese Cloisonné; English porcelain; Austrian enamel; German glass.

Hand-painted modern Meissen.

Hand-painted modern Meissen, flower subjects.

Hand-painted modern Meissen thimbles, with a French squirrel thimble-holder at the right.

Left: Graham Payne; right three: Jaspers of Yorkshire. All hand-painted.

Hand-painted thimbles. Left two: Jaspers; right two: Russell.

Hand-painted thimbles. Left two: Jaspers; right two: Russell.

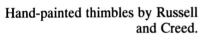

Privately made thimbles.

Hand-painted thimbles by Russell and Creed.

Left to right: London transport; Olympic Games; (right two) Russell and Creed.

Russell and Creed.

Left two: Russell and Creed; right
two: Wedgwood.

Left two: unknown; right two:
Russell and Creed.

Left two: Russell and Creed; right
two: transfer-printed unknown

Left: limited edition in the 1980s, artist unknown; center two: Russell and Creed; right: modern silver.

Left three: Wedgwood from the Kings and Queens of England series; right: Swann Comedy and Tragedy.

Left two: Wedgwood; right two: Russell and Creed.

Left two: Wedgwood Christmas pair; right two: Russell and Creed.

Left: Platt, a famous Royal Worcester painter; center left: unknown; right two: Russell and Creed.

All Wedgwood.

Transfer-printed Spode.

Transfer-printed Spode.

Transfer-printed Derby.

Left to right: Swann Queen's Jubilee; Swann Comedy and Tragedy; Swann TSL limited edition, gold and gem set for 10th anniversary by Helmut Greif; silver and enamel peep, Royal Wedding 12.12.92. by Woodsetton.

English silver and gem set, a special order and probably unique.

Another special order, probably unique English silver and gem set.

Silver and enamel thimble by Helmut Greif of Germany, one of the finest modern thimble makers. There is a charming thimble museum where he used to work in Creglingen. It is now run by his son.

Enamel from Austria.

Silver gilt and enamel by David Andersen, Norway.

Swann, silver and enamel cats.

Silver from Mexico.

A variety of thimbles. On the right is a glass and silver commemorative of Gorbachev.

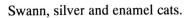

Silver and enamel thimble by Peter Swingler, one of the finest silver thimble makers

Left three: silver from Germany; right: Wedgwood, Queen Elizabeth II.

Enamel on brass peeps by Woodsetten containing tiny pictures of Royal Wedding and others.

Enamel on silver kingfisher by Peter Swingler.

Chinese cloisonné.

Enamel on silver: (left to right) Norway; England; Germany; England.

Enamel on silver, modern commemoratives, left three by Peter Swingler.

Enamel on silver. Left two: American; center right: German; right: English.

Enamel on silver, German souvenirs.

Advertising thimbles with jeweller's names, by Henry Griffiths, all c. 1930. These thimbles were probably given away with a purchase, but are now sought after fetching at least $70.

The "Oronsay" was part of a set of ships' names by Henry Griffiths, 1930. $160.

Single souvenir place name, also by Griffiths, of Southsea, an English holiday resort. All these large letter place names are avidly collected at $120 plus.

Several examples of English towns by Henry Griffiths, c. 1930. It is a good way to learn geography.

Still other English towns by Griffiths.

Rare ventilated thimble in plate with plastic lining c. 1910. Often the lining is missing. $120 plus.

Brass advertising thimbles, c. 1910/20, including some French. $25 each.

Brass and aluminum advertising thimbles, c. 1920/30. The one at the front right has a threader device. $20 each.

Three sewing compendiums, c. 1920. $40-70 each.

Aluminum advertising thimbles, c. 1930, including some from Russia.

Aluminum advertising thimbles, the third one showing a threader device.

Rare aluminum thimble with whistle advertising Monarch.

Aluminum advertising thimbles.

Whistle top in detail.

Silver advertising thimbles for jeweller's shops by Henry Griffiths, c. 1930. $70 plus.

20th Century Commemoratives:

Gold copy of 19th century Indian thimble by the Sfortzheim Museum.

Enamel on silver Queen Anne thimble, part of the series of British monarchs by Peter Swingler. Note the wonderful detailed enamelling on the top as well as the portrait.

Left three: modern Wedgwood; right: unnamed.

Thimbles brought out by TSL for the Queen's 60th birthday. Left and right: hand-painted porcelain; center: silver.

A set of thimbles to commemorate 50 years since the end of World War II by TSL, one for each armed service. This set is in porcelain.

The World War II commemorative set in silver.

Seven silver and enamel thimbles brought out by TSL on the unification of Europe, one for each country that joined.

Silver and gold gem set made by Helmut Greif to celebrate TSL's 10th anniversary.

Hand-painted thimbles, left three by Russell and Creed, right by the famous Platt.

At the right is Mrs. Thatcher, conservative Prime Minister, by Peter Swingler.

In the group the third thimble is Churchill by Peter Swingler.

Left two: Russell and Creed; center right: Mrs. Thatcher; right: Humphrey, the resident cat at 10 Downing Street.

Commemoratives for the
Queen's Silver Jubilee.

Commemoratives for the Queen's
Silver Jubilee.

Silver 1953 Queen Elizabeth II's Coronation. $220.

Above: Silver plate, Edward and Alexandra Coronation
1902. $350
Below: Silver with gold crown Coronation of George and
Mary, 1911. $420.

A more ornate version of the Coronation thimble with
coach and horses. $350.

Left to right: Silverplate thimble commemorating King George and Queen Mary's coronation; brass version; silver version; King George after Edward's abdication.

Red, white and blue enamel to commemorate the end of World War I. $250.

Four thimbles for Queen Elizabeth II's Coronation, 1953. Left to right: plate; silver; gold; silver. $500 for the gold.

King George and Queen Mary's Silver Jubilee. $350.

Plate commemorative thimble for Queen Elizabeth II's Coronation. $165.

Plate Edward and Alexandra Coronation commemorative thimble. $300.

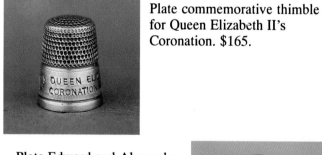

Left: Silver Wembley Exhibition, 1924; center: reverse of the same thimble in a slightly smaller version; right: Victorian thimble, 1887. $350.

Plate Edward and Alexandra Coronation commemorative thimble. $315.

Prince of Wales Investiture, silver and enamel commemorative thimble. $350, rare.

Reverse of Frost's wedding design.

Reverse showing date 1969.

Wedding of Charles and Diana, silver thimble by Mappen and Webb. Another fine modern thimble. $250.

Silver thimble by Shirley Frost for the wedding of Charles and Diana in 1981. An excellent example of modern design.

Enamel on silver, Silver Jubilee Queen Elizabeth II, 1977. $100 each.

Left three: Queen Elizabeth II's Silver Jubilee, 1977; right: Duchess of York and Princess Beatrice by Peter Swingler. $120-135 each.

Other Materials

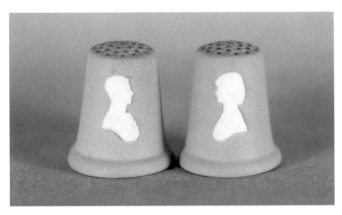

Charles and Diana's wedding by Wedgwood. $50.

Silver thimble by TSL to celebrate Queen Elizabeth II's 70th birthday in 1996 by A and J designs, two women silversmiths.$80.

English plastic thimbles of the 1930s.

Carved ivory animals from Kenya.

Copper and silver from Bath.

Reverse of Queen Elizabeth birthday thimble.

Left two: English porcelain with Celtic designs; right two: German glass.

Russian hand-painted thimbles. The left two are wood, the two are right porcelain. 1995.

Left three: Ivorine made in 1989; right: Chinese.

Left two: hand-painted wooden thimbles from Russia; right two: Wedgwood.

German glass.

All hand-painted wooden thimbles from Russia.

Left two: hand-painted wooden thimbles from Russia; right two: English thimbles.

The center two are from Scotland. Center left is horn and center right is colored and compacted heather stalks. The left thimble is brass and the right is silver and enamel.

Left to right: Graham Payne; Creed; two hand-etched glass, English thimbles.

Left two: English glass; right two: silver.

Bibliography

Benjamin, S. *English Enamel Boxes.* London: MacDonald Orbis, 1978.

Came, Richard. *Silver.* London: Weidenfeld & Nicolson.

Duchess d'Abrantes. *The Court of Napoleon.* Gloucester: Windrush, 1989

David, Rosalie. *The Pyramid Builders of Ancient Egypt.* London: University Press.

Delieb, Eric. *Investing in Silver.* London: Barrie & Rockliff, 1961.

Fraser, Antonia. *The Lives of the Kings and Queens of England.* London: Weidenfeld & Nicolson, 1975.

Golby. *Culture and Society in Britain, 1850-1890.* Oxford University Press.

Greif, Helmut. *Talks about Thimbles.* Austria: Fingerhut Museum Creglingen, 1984.

Harris, Godfrey. *The Fascination of Ivory.* Calif: The Americas Group, 1991.

Holmes, Edwin F. *A History of Thimbles.* London: Cornwall Books, 1985.

Jacksons. *English Goldsmiths and Other Marks.* Dover Press.

Jones, Owen. *The Grammar of Ornament.* London: Studio Editions, 1856.

Loe, A. *The Story of a Needle.* London: T. Nelson & Sons, 1880.

Oman, Charles. *English Engraved Silver 1150-1900.* London: Faber & Faber, 1978.

Payne, B. *History of Costume.* New York: Harper & Row, 1965.

Pelham Burn, Diane. *Sew Small.* Thimble Collectors International.

Phillips, J.M. *American Silver.* London: Max Parrish, 1949.

Rainwater, Dorothy T. *Encyclopedia of American Silver Manufacturers.* Penn: Schiffer, 1966.

Rainwater, Dorothy T. *American Jewelry Manufacturers.* Penn: Schiffer, 1988.

Rogers, Gay-Ann. *Illustrated History of Needlework Tools.* London: John Murray, 1983.

Rogers, Gay-Ann. *American Silver Thimbles.* London: Haggerston Press, 1989.

Sandon, Henry. *Royal Worcester Porcelain.* London: Barrie & Jenkins, 1973.

Spicer, Norma. *James Fenton.* Available through the Thimble Society.

Spicer, Norma. *James Swann.* Available through the Thimble Society.

Williams, A.R. & Maxwell Hyslop, K.R. *Ancient Steel from Egypt.* U.K.: Journal of Archaeological Science, No. 283-305, 1976.

Organizations of Interest to Collectors

Great Britain:

The Thimble Society
Grays Antiques
58 Davies Street
London W1Y 2LP
Great Britain

Tel/Fax: 0171 493 0560

Annual membership rates:
U.K.: £17 (1 year) - £32 (2 years)
Europe: £19 - £35
World Wide: £21 - £39

The Thimble Society

If you are interested in thimble collecting, do write to us for further information. If you have any thimbles or sewing tools to sell, again let us know for purchase or advice. If you have any photographs or information on rare thimbles please send it in and we will publish it. This book will be updated on a regular basis so new information is of great value to collectors.

Australia:

The Needlework Tool Collectors Society of Australia Ltd
L.P.O. Box 6025 Cromer
Victoria 3193
Australia

Annual membership rates:
Australia: $20
Overseas: $25

United States of America:

The Thimble Collectors International
Membership Chairman
8289 Northgate Drive
Rome, New York 13440-1941
USA

Annual membership rates
U.S.: $15
Worldwide: $20

The Netherlands:

The Dutch Thimble Association
Nederlandse Vingerhoedclub
P.O. Box 6427
7401 JK Deventer
The Netherlands

Annual membership: W.L.G: 37.50

Germany:

The Friends of the Thimble
Rund um den Fingerhut
c/o The Thimble Museum
Creglingen
Tauber River Valley
Germany

Maintenance and Conservation

Once you have started to collect thimbles you will certainly ask yourself what you should do to look after them and whether you should restore them.

Before you take a thimble to another collector, a dealer or a museum, you may be tempted to clean it, perhaps because you want to sell it, have it valued, or have it identified if you are uncertain of its origin and date. My general advice is to leave it alone. Over-cleaning can remove the attractive patina caused by age.

Plastic thimbles as advertising tools, U.S.A.

Thimble restoration should be undertaken only by experts, most of whom will decline to attempt extensive repairs and restoration work because heavily restored thimbles can look so much less attractive and their value is little enhanced if not actually reduced. Of course, the value of a restored thimble will never be the same as that of a perfect example. Good restoration work can be very expensive and the cost may be out of all proportion to the value of the thimble itself.

You will not need the services of a professional if the damage to your thimbles is only minor.

Ivory, Tortoiseshell, and Mother-of-Pearl Thimbles

Marks left on by sticky labels or general dirt can be easily removed with the impregnated wadding used to clean silver or brass. Never use a cleaner mixed with water - it will destroy the sheen. After you have rubbed the dirt off, restore the shine to the thimble with a drop of almond oil and buff it with a soft cloth. Tortoiseshell is best treated with almond oil or professionally polished. You will not be able to remove the yellow stains found on ivory - these are best tackled by an expert who will probably have to bleach them off very carefully.

Another tip for cleaning ivory is to make a paste of whitening and lemon juice. Rub this on the thimble and leave it to dry before removing the paste. Finally, polish the thimble with a soft cloth. Never clean ivory, bone, alabaster and other thimbles made of porous substances with detergent (which usually contains a mild bleaching agent) and water as you will remove the finish.

Chips and cracks on thimbles are best left alone unless you can find a restorer who specializes in ivory or tortoiseshell. Both materials can be professionally polished to remove surface scratches.

Ivory, tortoiseshell, and mother-of-pearl being natural substances, are affected by changes in temperature and can crack if the air is too dry; always put a glass of water near them. Ivory should be exposed to daylight occasionally to stop it yellowing, although not in direct sunlight. Mother-of-pearl can be professionally polished to restore sheen, but it is a delicate operation and not always successful, especially as it can reduce the dimpling effect.

Brass, Steel and Copper Thimbles

Modern cleaning agents can be used to clean nineteenth-century brass and copper. Earlier pieces, medieval thimbles for example, should not be cleaned. Their obvious age is part of their attraction. The old patina should always be retained. Repairs to early metal thimbles are not advisable either, because the metal is so brittle it can fall to pieces.

Steel thimbles should be handled as little as possible as they are particularly vulnerable to rust - even perspiration from fingers is enough to affect them. Rust can be retarded, if not prevented altogether, by rubbing some lubricating oil lightly onto the thimble. Cotton gloves should be worn if you are going to handle these thimbles frequently. Steel thimbles can be cleaned and polished by professionals, but it is expensive and they can end up looking very new with a rather flat appearance. Collectors look for the original bluish sheen and sparkling cut facets where applicable and will pay more for them.

Silver Thimbles

Do not use silver dip to clean a silver thimble with a gilt lining or any gilt decoration; if you immerse it in the dip you will plate it with the residue of silver collected in the dip and you will not be able to remove this plating. Avoid all silver cleaning compounds with even the smallest chrome content: although it will help to retard tarnishing, it will also plate the silver. If you have made this mistake, take your silver to a professional silver restorer who will be able to clean it up again.

The wholesale repair of silver thimbles is certainly best left to the professionals. Repairing damage to holes requires the removal of all stones beforehand as the thimble has to be heated to a very high temperature. Such heat will destroy any enamelled decoration or niello work. The repair process will also remove the patina on the thimble and the silver will need oxidizing again to regain its antique appearance. It is nearly impossible to repair stones and expensive to get new ones cut. Stone tops are virtually impossible to recreate.

Re-plating a silver or gold surface onto a base metal is usually possible. Remove any padding (in the case of a thimble holder) before immersing the item in the plating solution. You will end up with a very new-looking item. If you wish to re-plate only one piece of a set of sewing items, take the whole set to a professional silver restorer who will be able to match the color for you.

Silver-plating solutions can be bought fairly easily and work reasonably well if applied to a copper base but less well on brass. Such solutions need to be applied many times before the right appearance is obtained, but even then the plating is more likely to wear off than permanent plating undertaken by a professional.

Lead solder was often used to repair old silver. Any attempt to remove it may cause the item to disintegrate.

Thimbles by Spode with printed decorations

Gold Thimbles

Gold jewelry dip solutions can be bought and used to clean up gold thimbles. Thimbles set with porous stones such as turquoise, coral or pearl should not be immersed in such a solution; hard stones such as diamonds, sapphires and rubies, though, will come to no harm. All stones must be removed if repair work involves heating. Gold-plating costs at least twice as much as silver-plating and you will need to match the color closely; there are at least four different colors of gold - rose, green, yellow and "white". (The color of gold bears no relationship to its carat.)

The repair of a hole in the knurling of a gold (or silver) thimble must be done by a professional restorer and will be very expensive because the pattern of the knurling is so very difficult to reproduce. If you want to add a gold thimble to a set of a different color, you can plate gold on gold.

Porcelain and Glass Thimbles

Porcelain thimbles may have firing cracks. These are different from hairline cracks and they arise when the clay splits slightly during the firing process. Hairline cracks can develop from firing cracks so thimbles damaged in this way need particularly careful handling. Hairline cracks can be disguised to some extent by slight bleaching but this can damage painted motifs which will then have to be cleaned up and re-painted. If your thimbles are valuable, it is better not to restore them unless your restorer is an artist.

Local ceramic restorers may be a good option for repair work on porcelain thimbles which should not be washed because this may damage their painted surfaces and glazing.

Those of you lucky enough to have a silver thimble containing a minute scent bottle may have trouble removing the stopper. Put a few drops of lubricating oil around the neck of the bottle and leave it for at least a day - it may be necessary to repeat this process a number of times before you can finally loosen the stopper. A few drops of methyl alcohol can be used instead to remove any vestiges of perfume, before the stopper is eased out. If both these methods fail, immerse the bottle in hot water: the heated air inside the bottle will expand and help push the stopper out. Do not bend over the bottle to see what is happening as you may get a black eye. Use a wooden clothes peg - never metal pli-

ers which will cause chipping - if you must, to loosen the stopper.

Chips and rough edges on glass thimbles can be ground down to a smooth finish; cracks and breaks cannot be disguised though.

Wooden Thimbles

Do not attempt to clean painted wooden thimbles. They are protected by a thin layer of varnish (or less) which is their only defence against the elements. Dust them gently, but no more. Wooden thimbles are also affected by humidity and temperature changes: sensible storage and display are the best ways to limit damage. Try to avoid placing such thimbles in rooms that undergo great changes in temperature or under very strong, hot lighting.

Papier-mâché sewing boxes can be cleaned and their sheen restored with a paste made up of flour and almond oil. Leave the paste to dry and then rub it off gently. A silicon furniture spray or plain beeswax can also be used.

Cataloging and Photographing a Collection

Thimbles by Spode with printed decorations.

Fortunately not many thimble collections attract the attention of burglars. They prefer to take only videos, televisions and stereo cassette players: but many antiques and collectibles are now regarded as worth stealing. They may be difficult to trace. It is certainly worth keeping an up-to-date catalog of your collection, preferably with a photograph of each of your thimbles. These will help both you and the police to find them and provide the basis of any insurance claim you wish to make. You should also consider marking your thimbles with your postcode or zip code in an ultra-violet invisible ink. Numbering your thimbles is a good idea. Numbers should be written on sticky-backed labels if they are to be applied to porcelain or other porous materials such as ivory; otherwise numbers can be written directly onto metal thimbles with metal marker pens.

Your catalog will be both an invaluable record if you are burgled and a very useful means of showing other collectors and dealers the type and range of thimbles in your collection: you will not have to carry your whole thimble collection round with you wherever you go. The compilation of a catalog makes good sense and is satisfying in itself.

It is easiest to make your catalog up as your collections grows. A large ringed binder is a very convenient way of keeping records: each time you buy, sell or swap an item you can add or remove a page at will without interfering with the rest of the catalog - this is much more difficult if you have a conventional bound book. The entry for each thimble should mention its type (the material of which it is made), its size, any hallmarks or distinguishing features, its probable place and date of manufacture, any damage or flaws and anything you know about its previous ownership. You should also keep a "little black book" which matches your main book and lists when, where and from or to whom you bought or sold all your thimbles. You can keep all of your receipts in it too. For obvious reasons, you should conceal this book in a safe place.

Each thimble should ideally be illustrated with at least two photographs, since group shots of many thimbles together will not be particularly revealing of the fine distinguishing embellishments and ornaments on them. Thimbles of the same materials, design and date can however be photographed with each other and look very attractive together in pictures; group shots can also allow you to compare different designs immediately and conveniently. The major difficulty in such group shots is to get all the thimbles in focus.

Your photographs should show the thimbles' most notable features, "front" and "back" and perhaps inside, as well. It is of course up to the individual collector how much detail she or he wishes to show in the photographs. Ensure that you have sufficient depth of field to get the whole of your thimble in focus. You will need to stop down to F16 and may also have to use a light-sensitive "fast-film".

Thimbles are quite small objects and require photographing as close up as possible, with carefully positioned lighting; good natural daylight is best. Photograph them against plain or simple colored backgrounds. Metal thimbles, silver especially, can be adequately photographed using black-and-white film and may even look better in black-and-white than in color; the highly polished finish of some metal thimbles militates against using very strong lighting which can often be reflected and positioning is always repaid with better photographs. I always photograph through a "tent" which is lit from the outside. In truth, the tent is a white silk umbrella which is inverted over the thimble stand. It has a hole through which I push the camera's macro lens. All the lighting, perhaps two 500 watt floods, is positioned outside. This avoids glare and intensifies detail.

If you want to make slides for a talk, all you have to do is buy a roll of slide film. This is often called color transparency film. I like Fuji Velvia at a speed of 50 ASA for natural light. This film is expensive, but the color is very good. It is also made to use with indoor tungsten light. The film is then processed and mounted, so it is ready for showing.

Photographs will provide you with a record of your collection year by year and are useful in obtaining an up-to-date valuation. Valuations can be had from reputable thimble dealers and auction houses: all you need to do is take the relevant photograph, with any other information you may have, and the expert in question will provide you with a free verbal valuation. You will, however, have to pay some nominal fee if you require a valuation for insurance purposes. Many collectors are unaware of this service and more should take advantage of it. Reputable dealers and auction houses enjoy offering this service as it keeps them up to date with developments in the market-place and cements their relationships with potential clients among both new and well-established collectors. Collectors can equally enjoy the benefits of talking with an expert and learn about current prices. Valuations, even verbal, should be taken perhaps once a year and used if you are intending to update your insurance cover.

Display, Storage and Exhibition

In the course of my work as president of The Thimble Society of London and a thimble dealer and collector, I have enjoyed visiting many collections, public and private. No two individuals or institutions have displayed their collections in quite the same way. Some like to live and work (or sew) with their collection all around them, thimbles covering every spare inch of shelving and other surfaces. Others prefer to lock their thimbles away in drawers and bring them out only on special occasions. A friend of mine is so devoted to them that she cannot go away on holiday without taking some of her precious thimbles with her.

Showing a thimble collection to its best advantage presents an exciting challenge. A picture frame fitted over a shallow box containing small shelves can be glazed and hinged. The insides of the box and its shelves can be covered with velvet, and small

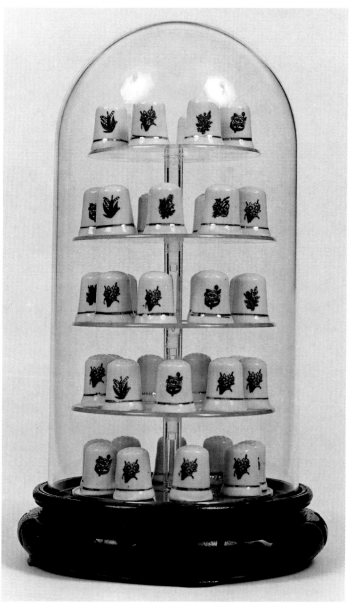

pieces of cork cut and stuck at intervals along the shelves to stop your thimbles wobbling each time the "door" is opened.

Glass domes fitted over round mounting shelves can be placed at either end of a mantelpiece, the domes themselves sitting on wood or lacquer bases stained or painted to suit the room. A glass-topped coffee table can be placed over a shallow showcase with thimbles on their side: use colored putty or children's plasticine to hold them in place.

Cotton reel drawers from an old sewing cabinet are ideally partitioned for thimble display; these can be bought in antique markets or occasionally picked up from stores undergoing complete re-fitting and re-furbishing. Printer's wooden trays also make attractive display units. These can be fitted with a glass or perspex door with light brass hinges, when used up-right, or laid flat on a made-to-measure wrought iron or brass coffee table frame and then covered with a glass top.

You should display your thimbles as you like and to reflect your taste and lifestyle. If you have young children, pets or visitors who are likely to knock thimbles to the floor or otherwise damage them, it may be best to keep them in locked glass display cases or cabinets. These will protect your collection and save you having to dust them quite so often. How you group them, whether by nationality, date or material is your choice.

Many major and small museums have thimbles and sewing accessories such as sewing sets, pincushions and thimble cases on display that are of interest to thimble collectors, almost as much for the manner of display as for the actual thimbles themselves.

Thimbles that you choose not to display can be stored away in drawers, wrapped in acid-free tissue paper. This will prevent tarnishing on silver thimbles. The packaging on silver thimbles should not be secured with elastic bands as the pressure from them can leave black marks on silver. A small cachet of camphor crystals placed close to silver thimbles will also help to prevent them from tarnishing if they are on display in a cabinet.

Porcelain thimbles stored in cotton wool can get so hot during the summer that the paint on them becomes sticky. If this happens, do not remove the cotton wool, but let the thimbles cool at room temperature (you can even put them in a 'fridge later to harden the paint again). Finally, remove any material stuck to them by moistening them slightly.

When you travel with your thimbles, pack them carefully so that there is no chance of them chipping or smashing against each other, the heavier coarser ones against the more delicate and fragile ones especially. If you attend thimble society meetings and fairs, or frequent antique markets with any of your thimbles, make sure that you have adequate all-risk or travel insurance cover for them. You can now buy custom made small travelling cases with tiny compartments inside to house each thimble. They cost around $100 and can be ordered through the Thimble Society and other outlets.

I do hope that you have enjoyed accompanying me around the world of thimbles. The information contained in this book should give you some help towards forming your own exciting collection. Thimble collecting celebrates the small, the useful, the beautiful, and the precious, along the companionable part of our lives. So do join us. Here is wishing you good luck and good hunting.